YOU SPEAK GOOD ENGLISH FOR A NIGERIAN

OREOLUWA ARMY

Copyright © 2020 Oreoluwa Army

The events and conversations in this book have been set down to the best of the author's ability, although some names have been changed to protect the privacy of individuals. All rights reserved. No portion of this book may be reproduced in any form without permission from the publisher, except as permitted by U.S. copyright law. For permissions contact:

oreolujasmine@yahoo.com

Cover Art by Mayowa Alabi.

ISBN: 978-1-7349497-0-4 (ebook)
ISBN: 978-1-7349497-1-1 (Paperback)

To my darling girl, Keeva, may you have the courage
to pursue your dreams and do phenomenal things.

To my super-husband, Mike,
you'll always be my Lord RedBeard.

ACKNOWLEDGMENTS

Thank you to my husband, Mike, for his addition and hard work editing parts of my manuscript.

Thank you to my brother, Leke, for his input on the cover design.

Thank you to all my friends and family who encouraged me to share a bit of my immigration experience.

CONTENTS

Acknowledgments v
1. Leaving Home 1
2. Divisions and Connections 11
3. Friends Make the World Go Round. 19
4. Seasons of Change. 31
5. What's in a Name? 37
6. Green Pasture. 47
7. *Oyinbo* 61
8. Immigrant Mentality 87
9. Rural Racism 99
10. Black vs. Black 105
11. Sanity vs. Insanity 117
12. You Speak Good English for a Nigerian 127
13. The Thief of Gratitude 131
14. Stranger Than Strange 137
15. A Faith-based Journey 151

LEAVING HOME

I REMEMBER MY FIRST TIME in Boston Logan airport. I had just arrived to the United States and had nowhere to stay. It was late afternoon as I sat in the arrival area with four heavy bags crushed against me, trying to block out the buzz of activity, so I could figure out what to do next.

I'd dreamt of that day for years. Of leaving my country for another in search of better opportunities. In search of a different life. In search of a new path.

I'd gotten my student visa two months earlier and every day since, each time I lay my head to sleep, I was bombarded with thoughts of what would happen when I got to America.

What would it be like? Would I adapt well to the environment? Would it change me? How would it change me? Would I like it? Would I hate it? Would I regret leaving my home country?

I never used to have trouble falling and staying asleep. My parents would often tease me by calling me Jonah because Jonah was a character in the Bible who fell into a deep sleep on a ship in the midst of a raging storm. But after getting my student visa, the sheer excitement of the possibilities, the unknowns, and the planning ahead of me—all of it kept me awake at night.

I have to change my naira to dollars. I have to figure out where to live. I have to book a flight. How would schooling in America be? Would I succeed? Would I find food I can eat there?

Those two months of restless nights still flew by. I was busy with work during the day and planning my trip at night. I moved my life savings from various investments to my savings account, bought my plane ticket and soaked up the last bits of scorching Nigerian sun. I spent my weekends visiting close friends one last time before my departure and packed my travel bags. There was a lot of weighing and reweighing each time I put in something new. I struggled deciding what I needed to take with me to America.

I've always been very prudent with money. My parents worked as bankers for nearly three decades. My mom specifically taught me and my siblings how to save and the importance of doing it. Every time she gave me money for school, she'd say, "Buy only the necessities!" My mom believes in saving and investing in stocks, and in setting money aside regularly to fall back on during the rainy days. My dad, on the other hand, believes in spending money whenever you have it. "Why deprive yourself of what you want if you have the money to get it now?" he'd ask. Let's just say I saw the wisdom in and the results of my mom's way firsthand, and I wisely chose to follow that path.

Beyond being a saver, I've always been a planner too. I've had a picture of what I want my life to be since I was a teenager. I had dreams of things I wanted to do and who I wanted to be. Some of those dreams changed as I grew older, some were edited and some fine-tuned. But one of them always remained—my desire to leave Nigeria and study abroad.

As soon as I got my student visa, I was so happy. It was one step closer to fulfilling my plans. I immediately started my search for housing. My new school was in Boston and had on-campus housing for international students. I did not consider that as an option because it cost a lot more than what I wanted to spend on accommodation. I browsed through Craigslist even though I had heard nothing but bad news about the site.

My school happened to have a section on their website listing alternative housing options for international students to explore. One of them was a house for girls on Newbury Street in Boston. It was run by the Unitarian Universalist Urban Ministry. It looked promising. I reached out to them, and they encouraged me to apply, informing me that they would get back to me to let me know if I was accepted or not.

The Ministry's housing application required a short essay about why I wanted to live there and what social justice meant to me, along with two landlord references. After I submitted the application, I was told they would have to review my application and have a Skype interview with me before making a decision. I shared my arrival schedule and was disappointed when they said they wouldn't have decided by then.

At that time, every other aspect of my trip was planned out except where I was going to live. I knew if push came to shove I could stay in a hotel for a few days while I figured things out, but I didn't want to start out my student journey by spending so much on a hotel. From my rough estimate, a hotel stay for a week in Boston would have been as much as one month's rent, so I dreaded that option. But it was an option, nonetheless.

An old classmate of mine, Femi, who was studying in Philadelphia knew of another old classmate, Hamed, who was studying in Boston. He gave me Hamed's number and encouraged me to ask him for advice on accommodation. So I did.

Hamed knew of a girl who was getting ready to resume school in Boston around the same time I was, but she was still in Nigeria. I reached out to her, and we talked briefly on the phone. She told me she had a sister in Nevada whom she was going to visit before traveling to Boston. According to her schedule, she was going to arrive in Boston a day after me. She did not have concrete plans regarding housing at that point, but she had friends in Boston with a possible spare room she planned to rent when it became available. In the meantime, she had made plans to stay with an Indian girl for a few days till the other space was available. I'm not sure how she knew the Indian girl, but my guess was she must have known her through the international student portal at the school she would attend that fall.

The involvement of friends of friends of friends in reaching a goal is common for Nigerians. Word-of-mouth referrals for help is something I was used to, and I especially appreciated this insight as I looked for reasonable living options in what would become my new home.

My Nigeria-Boston connection offered to ask the Indian girl if I could also stay in the room with her for a few days. She reported back that the Indian girl agreed at the rate of $100 a day. I accepted the offer since it was less than a week until my trip, and I didn't have any other promising leads.

A few months later, and after becoming accustomed to the American currency, I realized how unfair that Indian girl had been to charge that kind of amount as a daily rate. In retrospect, I could have rented a cheap hotel at that price, or one that at least offered a complimentary breakfast. When I had converted that amount to naira, it had seemed like a lot to pay for just one night's stay in someone's apartment. But then at the time $1 was about 170 naira, so I couldn't use that as a good gauge of what $100 really was. It annoyed me to think that she'd taken advantage of me. I'm the type of person that if the roles were reversed, I would have accommodated that Indian girl, or anyone else in a similar situation as I was in, for free. And I would have done it for at least a couple of days while they found their feet in a strange place.

So, there I was sitting in the airport with my heavy luggage, waiting for a text from an Indian girl I did not know, telling me what time to show up so she could let me into her apartment.

I do not remember my Nigeria-Boston connection's name since we did not end up being friends, so I'll call her Bisi.

Bisi had given me the Indian girl's number, and I had saved it for my arrival in Boston. As soon as I arrived at Boston Logan airport, I sat down with my luggage and sent the Indian girl a text message letting her know I had arrived and asking where I should go.

While waiting for her reply, I saw some international student representatives from Northeastern University welcoming new international students, and I was tempted to go with them just to end the waiting game. But I knew that wouldn't help at all. I still didn't know where I would be staying, and I assumed those students being welcomed were undergraduates who would be living on campus. With an unexpected request from a graduate student who would be living off campus, they probably would have looked at me like, "Sorry we can't help you."

After what felt like eternity (but was actually about two hours), I got a reply from the Indian girl saying she was leaving class shortly. She sent me the address to her apartment, saying I could head over.

As soon as I had a destination, I dragged my bags outside the airport and got a cab to take me to Allston. The address led me to a three-story red brick building. The door to the building itself was open, but there was another door inside the foyer leading up to the apartments that was locked, so I waited on the steps outside. I made sure that I sat at one corner of the steps, so I wasn't blocking anyone from entering. Now that I think of it, I am so glad it wasn't a cold fall day as it sometimes is in the Northeast in late August. I'm glad it wasn't a rainy one either.

Instead, it was a nice, sunny fall day, so my two-hour wait on those steps wasn't as terrible as it could have been. I'm not much of a people watcher, but being in America for the first time, there was a lot to observe and take in.

I observed white people as they walked down the street, taking in their style of dress. It was much different from the colorful fabrics that were a core part of the Nigerian culture. Why were the women's shorts so short? I wondered. I was seeing parts of their buttocks on display that I would rather not be seeing. I saw large tattoos displayed on people's arms the likes of which I hadn't seen before. I watched cars drive by without raising dust. I did not hear the noise of cars honking angrily at each other every two seconds, nor did I hear insults and curses flying from bus conductors and bus passengers as they galloped around town in rickety buses. It was quiet. The atmosphere seemed calm and peaceful.

A couple of hours later the Indian girl showed up. She introduced herself, but I'm terrible with names so it did not stick. She held the door open while I moved my bags into the building, then we walked up two flights of stairs to her two-bedroom apartment. I had to take two trips down the stairs to transport all of my luggage into the apartment. The Indian girl showed me to the vacant room. Then I realized that I was tired and quite jetlagged.

That morning, I had flown into Boston from New York because I had chosen an indirect flight from Lagos to New York, arriving the night before. I'd added a flight to Boston for the following morning to save on cost. That meant I had to book a hotel in New York until my next-morning flight, and I had to take a taxi from the airport. It was an absolute mess. In Nigeria, we generally do not seek out online reviews of places. We usually rely more on word-of-mouth testimonies of places and businesses, so I did not think to check the online reviews about the hotel I was booking. I just found the cheapest available hotel and booked it expecting that it would be good enough. It was in America after all.

While I was in the taxi, I wondered why it was taking so long to get there, and my heart rate kept climbing higher as the meter reading rose. I'd only heard about taxi meters in movies when one of the characters would say to the taxi driver, "Keep the meter running." I did not know what that really meant until I was sitting in a New York taxi for the first time. I kept one eye on the meter the whole ride to the hotel. I briefly wondered if the taxi driver was taking a longer route on purpose. It just seemed so far! Later I would shake my head at my own silliness and wonder why I had not properly researched the distance of the airport to the hotel and factored in the cost of a taxi ride. I would have gotten a more expensive hotel closer to the airport, which would have cost the same as the cheaper hotel plus the taxi ride.

After almost forty-five minutes, we arrived at the hotel, and I discovered it was a low-end place in an area referred to as Chinatown. I paid the taxi driver and lugged my bags up one flight of stairs to the check-in counter.

I took the bags containing important documents with me and left the others near the entrance, praying no one would steal them.

It was a weird hotel. It was sitting atop a shop of some sort, so I had to go up one set of stairs before finding the check-in counter. There was an Indian man there, and I told him I had a reservation. He checked me in, and I asked him if I could get some help with my bags. He said no, he was the only one there, and he couldn't leave the desk. I did not see anyone else waiting to check in, so it wasn't like he was the busiest man at that moment, but I held my tongue and got my bags myself. Luckily it was only one flight of stairs. When I returned with all my bags, he mentioned that there was a locker I could keep my bags in to avoid carrying them all the way up another flight of stairs to my room.

The locker had a self-service lock and key, so I stored the bags with non-essential items in there for the night and went up to the room. The room was even weirder. It could not fit two people comfortably. It would not even fit a large person comfortably. The bed was right next to the door. I could sit on the bed and reach the door handle. The bed was a twin size, and I had not been given any toiletries. Apparently it was one of those bring-your-own-toiletry types of hotel.

I woke up at 3 a.m. that night because my body was still running on Nigerian time. It would take a week for my body to get the memo about the change in time zones. Since I was awake, I decided to do some research online. I discovered that I could schedule an airport shuttle for a flat fee, which was cheaper than what I had paid for a taxi. I used that option for my ride back to the airport, and I was soon on my way to Boston.

While waiting for Bisi to arrive to the Indian girl's apartment, I had gone looking for food. According to my parents, I have been a picky eater since I was a baby. Even as an adult, many foods don't appeal to me. It doesn't matter how hungry I am, I can easily choose to go without food rather than try something that does not look or smell appealing to me.

I saw an Italian restaurant next door and decided to be brave. I walked up to the counter and looked up at the menu. Nothing looked familiar. I did not understand anything on the menu. Everything seemed strange. I saw something that had chicken and salad in the name and decided to try it. Those were familiar words. I placed my order and when it was ready, I walked back to the apartment with it. I opened it with dread, hoping I had not just wasted my money on something I would not be able to eat. I had thought I couldn't go wrong with salad. I was wrong. This was not salad as I knew it. This was far from Nigerian salad. What I saw were large chunks of lettuce, some white stuff, and baby tomatoes. And some liquid that I assumed was supposed to go on the salad.

Disappointing.

I would find out years later that the white stuff was feta cheese and the liquid was salad dressing. In Nigeria, we shred our lettuce to much smaller bits than anywhere I've seen in America. American lettuce shreds are sized so a human can only put one shred into their mouths for a comfortable bite. I'm always baffled when I see people awkwardly forking huge lettuce leaves into their mouths and wonder why restaurants don't cut them into smaller bits. Also, we eat salad with salad cream, though some people use mayonnaise, which I find odd. But I find eating salad with just salad dressing even odder.

I ended up throwing the salad in the trash. I could almost hear my mom yelling at me for being wasteful: "Some people don't have food to eat, yet here you are wasting food!" Luckily the meal had come with a bread roll, which I was able to eat. The chicken had ended up in the trash too. It was too bland for me. I was used to well-seasoned food. I often wonder if I would feel differently eating that meal again today. But to a girl eating a meal far stranger than anything she'd ever had before, it was terrible.

An hour later, I decided to take another walk to look for food and found a small mom-and-pop grocery store near the bus stop. I went in and there, I found hope. I found bread—nothing like the bread back home, but at least it was familiar and, I hoped, edible. I got some butter, milk, sugar, and tea. The milk we have in Nigeria is the dry, powdered kind, so it was strange buying liquid milk, but that was all that was available. Armed with my stash, I walked back to the apartment and made some very familiar bread and tea. I had bread and tea for breakfast, lunch, and dinner that day.

Ah, a full day in America conquered.

Bisi finally arrived in Boston late that evening. It was the first time I'd met Bisi in person. She was friendly enough but a little too bossy for my liking.

The next morning, I had more bread and tea. Thankfully for lunch, Bisi suggested we go to one of the larger grocery stores to buy stuff to cook stew with. We took the train to the store and bought some tomatoes, vegetable oil, rice, seasoning, and salt, then went back to the apartment. The Indian girl and her roommate had given us a spare key so we could move in and out freely.

Together, Bisi and I cooked some rice and stew for lunch. I was glad not to have to eat bread and tea all day again. The next day we took the train to see the college where she would be getting her master's degree. Meanwhile, I had been making calls about possible places to live. The Indian girl reminded us that we had to leave by Monday. Bisi's explanation of the situation was that the Indian girl and her roommates' lease was expiring the next week, so they wanted us gone by Monday to avoid issues with the landlord. They were just trying to make some quick money from us before then.

I checked online for available listings not too far from my college and made a few calls. I had an appointment to tour one apartment, but the other person chose not to show up and did not have the courtesy to let me know ahead of time, so I ended up walking about half an hour to the meeting point then walking back "home." By Thursday, I had toured only one apartment.

Early on Friday morning, I received an email from one of the managers of the off-campus house run by the Universalist Unitarian Urban Ministry. I had applied a month earlier, but they were asking if I was available for a Skype interview. I said yes, and we set up a time for later that morning.

The interview went well, and she said she would get back to me once she spoke with the director of the program. The housing was run to provide affordable accommodation for young women who were studying in Boston. They were able to keep the cost far below the typical rent for downtown Boston.

Later that afternoon, I got the good news that my application had been approved. I was so relieved. After five days in the US, I finally had a place to stay. A place I would call home for the next few years.

DIVISIONS AND CONNECTIONS

RACIAL STEREOTYPES ARE A PART of life. There are stereotypes about every race, some untrue and others downright ridiculous. Although I must admit, a handful of them are true, but even those that are true don't necessarily apply to every member of that race.

When I told a friend at work I was moving to the US for graduate school, the first thing he said was "be careful, white people have guns, and they can shoot you if you make them angry." The second thing he said was "white people don't like Black people." I'm glad I haven't been shot by a gun-wielding white person, and although I have met my share of racist, intolerant, narrow-minded white people, my experience with white people is that they are like every other human from every other race.

September 1, 2014 had me dragging my massive luggage across town from Allston to Boston to move into what would be my home for the next three years. Bisi offered to help me move. She was moving in with friends that morning too. With her help, we were able to load up our bags onto the train. When we got to our stop, we tried to make quick work of getting our bags down to avoid causing delays. That took some work since we probably had seven bags between us.

As we were trying to get control of all of the bags, a white woman who was also getting off stopped to give me a hand as she saw me struggle to get all my bags off the train. She smiled as she lifted my bags onto the pavement. I thanked her profusely. It was an unexpected gesture from a stranger. And a white one at that. Although I didn't believe the stereotype that white people went about shooting everyone they were angry with, a part of me wondered if white people really hated Black people. Growing up in a country where I'd only seen probably five white people in my life, I didn't know a lot about white people or white culture except what I saw on TV. And I have never been the type to believe what I see on TV.

Although a seemingly small, albeit kind gesture, having that white woman help me with my bags that day made a lasting impression on me. Of course, since then I've had a lot of positive interactions with white people in general—I've had white men and women hold doors open for me, compliment my outfits, and so on. Nevertheless, experiencing that act of kindness in my second week in America made me realize one important fact: white people are just another racial group in the human race. There are just as many nice, kind, giving, loving white people as there are nice, kind, giving, loving Blacks, Latinos, Asians, or Middle Easterners. On the other hand, there are just as many horrible, racist, mean, brutal white people as there are those kinds of people in every other race.

It's clear to me that stereotypes do more to divide people than bring them together.

As a young girl, I had friends from different tribes of Nigeria. It was always disappointing to hear parents tell their children not to be friends with someone from a particular tribe because of their personal dislike for that tribe. In most cases, the parents' personal dislike was never as a result of personal experience, but merely due to some preconceived notion that they have always had that certain tribes are not to be trusted.

If I always believed the stereotypes that other members of my Yoruba tribe held, there would have been a lot that I missed. As I grew older, I was interested in learning about other tribes and cultures including their foods and traditions. I had a few Igbo friends, and some of them taught me how to make a couple of Igbo soups which quickly became my favorite.

I had that same mentality of embracing other traditions when I arrived in the US. I don't dislike my fellow Nigerians, but I never had the desire to seek out a Nigerian clique. Growing up and living among Nigerians and Black people, I wanted to mix with people of different cultures and backgrounds so as to learn about their cultures, traditions, and languages. I had started learning Spanish when I was seventeen after listening to the Spanish version of Mario Vazquez's song, "Galleria." I memorized the lyrics to "Galleria," and eventually I subscribed to receive free online Spanish audio lessons by somebody named Marcus Santamaria. There was no one to practice Spanish with because I didn't know anyone interested in learning a new language with me. I didn't get a lot of practice, but I still kept listening to my audio lessons and learning new sentences in Spanish. After moving to Boston, a few of my housemates were Latinas, so I would ask them to speak to me in Spanish so I could learn. And let's just say it very different from listening to audio lessons!

I grew up as a Christian in Nigeria, so after a week of settling into my new home in Boston, I was ready to begin my search for a church. I googled "churches near me" one Sunday, and I saw that there was a church a few blocks up the street from where I lived, so I decided to check it out. It was a Baptist church, and although I attended a Pentecostal church back in Nigeria, I was open to checking it out, so I went in. After about fifteen minutes of the service, I was ready to leave. I'd found a pamphlet on the chair, and when I turned to the back, there was a declaration about how the church supported homosexual marriage and was even willing to conduct homosexual marriage ceremonies.

Since when do churches do that? I thought. I was shocked.

My understanding of the Scriptures was that although we are to love everyone unconditionally, we are not to condone, encourage, or partake in things that God, through His word, clearly stated as sinful. *Who are we to pick and choose what part of the Scripture to obey? Who are we to decide what portion of the Scripture applies in these present times and what does not?* I was dismayed.

The rejection of this church's doctrine may seem odd to those who don't believe, like atheists and agnostics who don't believe that God exists. And many may believe that Christianity and other religions are lies set to brainwash people. Since those individuals they don't believe in the first place, it is understandable that they would also not believe the Bible. On the other hand, for someone who claims to believe in God, reads the Bible and follows its standards, and claims to be a Christian, how such a person could disregard all that and still support something God is clearly against (per the Bible) is beyond me. The leader on the pulpit announced that it was time for communion, and I decided that it was time to leave. I was not going to take communion in that church. I quickly got up and left.

Google showed me that there was another church a block down, and I decided to give that one a try. It was an old Baptist church. I went in and observed the people around. I read the church newsletter. No strange doctrine as far as I could tell, so I stayed till the end of the service and walked back home after. The next time, I changed my Google search to "Pentecostal churches near me." I found a few options, and the next Sunday I visited one in Cambridge. It was predominantly Black with only one or two white people there. It felt familiar, but I did not want familiar. I wanted my food to be familiar, not my life's experiences.

There was a post–Sunday service breakfast organized for first-time guests in the downstairs of the church. The introvert in me wanted to leave right away and go home instead, but I silenced her and decided to attend. I met a few friendly people, in particular one young Nigerian lady. From her name I could tell she was from my tribe. She told me she had also come to the US to attend Harvard a few years ago. She was now a working professional and told me to reach out to her if I needed someone to talk to as she understood how lonely and discouraging it could sometimes be in a new environment without family or close friends around. I thanked her and took her number, but I never reached out to her. I always feel unsure when people say things like that. I'm never sure if they are just trying to be nice or if they really mean what they say. I've always been able to lift myself out of loneliness and discouragement, so I never really had a reason for reaching out to her.

I liked the church well enough, but I did not go back there. I wanted a diverse church. I wanted fellowship with people who were not like me—people that were from different cultures and races. I visited a few churches before I eventually found one that was diverse and taught biblical doctrines. It was such a joy to worship God with other believers, people from different tribes and languages and skin colors. I attended the church for almost a year until I started to notice certain doctrines that were a little too extreme for my comfort level.

When I learned that one of their core beliefs was that only people who attended their church would make it into Heaven, I had to leave. I had to disconnect myself from the friends I had made there who were so invested in the church and its beliefs. That was a tough decision to make because I had really liked the church. I had enjoyed the fellowship, joking around, and breaking bread with the diverse bunch at the church. But it had started to feel more like a cult than a church. So, for my own peace of mind, I broke away from it.

A few months later, I found another church, but it wasn't as diverse. I was one of three Black people there. I reasoned to myself that maybe it was best to focus on a church with sound doctrine rather than diversity. I am comfortable enough in my skin to not mind being the only Black person in a gathering, but it's always nice to not always stand out as the only one. While I was getting ready to move to the US, I did not think finding a good church would be as challenging as it proved to be.

Before moving to the US, I rarely thought about how much racism there was in the world. Unfortunately, I am now painfully aware and think about it daily. When I see yet another news story of a Black person killed or maltreated for no just reason by a white police officer, it makes me wonder what kind of hatred must be coursing through their veins. Although I live in a part of the country that does not experience as much of the senseless killing of Black people by police officers that some American cities, I have occasionally wondered what would happen if I encountered someone in authority that was blatantly racist toward me.

Since becoming a mother (more on that later), I've had a mental image in my head a few times of me driving with my baby in the back seat and getting pulled over by a police officer that just hates the sight of me because of my skin color. I imagine him asking me to get out of the car, which I hesitate to do because my baby in the car is my priority. I imagine telling him I cannot leave my baby unattended in the car, and he interprets it as resisting authority and things go downhill from there.

In another image, I see myself complying and getting out of the car, and all of a sudden he's putting handcuffs on me for no reason. Then I start to fight because I'm being handcuffed with my baby in the car. *How do I know she will be safe? How do I know what will happen to her? How do I know what they will do to her? Can I call my husband to come get her before they take me away without my child?*

These images played in my head while driving to work one day after hearing of yet another senseless attack on a Black person with a baby. They were tackled by cops while running away from them after being pulled over. I don't know if that person was innocent, but that baby was. *Why would anyone in their right minds tackle someone who's holding a baby?* I'm not a police officer, but shouldn't there be more training on how to de-escalate a situation to ensure minimal harm to innocent people?

I imagine being a police officer is a high-stress job, but my impression of most of them is that they are too trigger hungry and always quick to use brute force even when it is unnecessary. It is no wonder that many Black Americans are angry, on edge, and distrustful of everything white. One of my housemates in Boston hated white cops so much that she would go on and on about it. One day she asked me what I thought. I shrugged. She proceeded to tell me about the Black Lives Matter movement and how she was a strong advocate for it. She asked, "'Can you believe how those white people are making it about them too by saying 'all lives matter'?" I wanted to say, "Hey, I'm still fresh from Nigeria. I pretty much just got here, so I don't even know what's been going on." But all I did was listen so I could understand what was going on better.

I generally don't follow the news because it always seems to be all negative. But some of the news trickles into social media, so I end up seeing some of it. Much of the bad news is the result of conflict among polarized groups. In America, there are different people from different backgrounds, with different cultures and practices. Within those backgrounds and cultures, the differences can deepen as humans experience internal conflicts as well. I experienced the shock of new religious conflicts firsthand with my search for a church that aligned with my doctrine-based religious upbringing. I've since come to believe that the church should love and accept everyone. But I still struggle when a church changes to accommodate societal standards by rejecting what I believe to be the foundational principles of Christianity found in the Bible. Yet, in another church, I grew uncomfortable when it became too cult-like. My own search for a place of ideological belonging was difficult. I believe this all demonstrates the complexities each of us faces within our backgrounds, cultures, and practices. But as we grow, educate ourselves, and encounter people with ideologies and realities outside our realm of comfort, we need to ask ourselves if our hesitation to understand their ideologies and realities is caused by cultural beliefs or societal bias.

In Nigeria, there is always some tribal conflict or the other that goes on because some people believe their tribe to be superior to others. And that's a country in which nearly everyone is of the same race. It really is sad and discouraging to see all the hatred some white people have for Black people, and the hatred some Black people have for white people, especially in America.

It doesn't surprise me that in America, a country full of people from different races, we'll have cultural conflicts as well. But seemingly profound differences that drive these conflicts make us lose sight of our commonalities. In the US, the conflicts are beyond cultural or tribal levels. The problem here is that one race believes itself to be superior to the other, while seeking the annihilation of the other race. I cannot understand the hatred. We are all humans of the same race—the human race. We all bleed the same. We are exactly the same inside and out except for the color of our skin. So, what's all the hatred for?

FRIENDS MAKE THE WORLD GO ROUND

I AM AS PICKY ABOUT my friends as I am about my food. I am friendly, but I don't make friends very easily. I'm generally respectful of people, but I don't have to be friends with someone to respect them. I've always held the belief that not everyone is meant to be my friend, just as I am not meant to be friends with everybody. Not everybody likes me, and I don't like everybody I come across.

I do have a few friends that I wanted to write about because they have been so crucial to my story. Why have I singled these people out? I cannot imagine my life without their influence. These are just a few of the valuable people I have in my life. Listing them all and their impact in my life would require a whole book. Not one of them has been a negative influence on me. As a personal rule, I don't give room for any negative influence in my life or in my mind. The importance of choosing the right people to be friends with cannot be overstated. Of course there are many others who in one way or the other have impacted my life and still continue to impact my life. But the friends I feature here have consistently added value to my life, and I can only hope that I have added value to theirs too.

My new university had a website for international students who were looking for roommates. We could create a profile to post adverts and connect with each other in the hopes of finding a potential fit. During my search for housing those first few days in Boston, I had created a profile and reached out to a few people, hoping to find a roommate. That was how I met Temi. From her name I could tell she was Nigerian.

Temi arrived in Boston about a week and a half after I did. She reached out to me via the housing site and asked if I already had a place and if she could be my roommate, or if I would be willing to rent an apartment together with her. I told her I had just gotten a place to live in, and that it was not the type I could have a roommate in since people who lived in the house had to go through an application process and a selection process. I encouraged her to apply, but she preferred to live where she would have more freedom.

It's not that I didn't have freedom in my housing situation, but it was similar to a girls' hostel on campus, and with that came a few rules. One rule was that male guests had to be out of the building by 10 p.m. and could not be in before 10 a.m. They were not allowed into the bedrooms—they were only allowed in the common areas such as the living rooms and the dining areas. I didn't mind the rules; I was there to study hard and save money while I was at it. And I appreciated not having men in my private living spaces. If I had rented a different type of apartment with a roommate, I would not have a say in male companions being around at different times of the day. Who knows what I would have stumbled upon while getting up to pee in the middle of the night! I appreciated the rules in place in my house.

Temi told me when she would be arriving in Boston and asked if we could meet. I mentioned that when I first tried going to the campus, I had gotten lost in it, so I was willing to help her navigate the sprawling campus. We agreed to meet there. I have not for once regretted meeting Temi. She is such a delight.

Temi and I are very different, yet we complement each other well. She is very friendly and outgoing, while I am the opposite. She is a total extrovert and, being an introvert, her bubbly spirit wears me out sometimes. We have a lot of memories from our graduate school experience, and sometimes we would reminisce over our broke college days and those tough discouraging periods when we didn't know where our next tuition payment would come from. We also called each other at night lament over being single, and to talk about how hard it was to meet sane, sensible men who were not trying to just get into our pants.

Temi and I would encourage each other when funds from Nigeria were not forthcoming. The naira kept weakening, and it was difficult to keep up with tuition payments. Our student accounts were locked on more than one occasion after we failed to meet our payment deadlines. We would walk together to the student account department to plead with them to remove the holds so we could register for courses for the following semester. It was our way of offering each other moral support.

Although stressful while living through it, Temi and I would laugh at those times in the years to come. It was such a miserable period, but we were able to encourage each other through it. Not once did we encourage each other to do anything illegal or immoral. There is nothing like a friend with whom you can walk through tough times with some joy and still be able to find things to laugh about. We were able to constantly remind each other of the blessings we had, and that there was always that light at the end of the tunnel. Temi was my link to the Nigerian community in Boston. She attended a Nigerian church and invited me a few times to their Sunday services. I had a church I was attending regularly at the time, but I agreed to go once. The service was alright. It was exactly like being in Nigeria on a Sunday morning.

A few weeks after the fall 2014 semester resumed, Temi got an on-campus job and encouraged me to apply for the same position. I did but it took me longer to get a response. Temi kept encouraging me, sure that it would work out. A month later I got the job. Not once have I ever felt that she did not have my back or that she tried to sabotage me in any way.

It's true that many people feel that by helping others they are somehow sabotaging themselves. Some people even believe that staying focused on themselves is the only way for them to get ahead in life. I've experienced that so many times. People have tried to cut me down and have withheld vital information, thinking somehow if they help me, they will somehow end up behind. That's such a terrible lie that people allow into their heads. By genuinely helping someone without expecting anything in return, you're not going to end up behind. If you keep working hard, helping someone else to be successful will not derail your own success. In fact, by helping others you'll be sowing good seeds for your own future.

Temi and I would drag each other along to attend all the international student immigration pathway forums on campus. These were tedious meetings where we learned the next steps for work visas or other immigrant visas. We knew we did not want to go back to Nigeria after all the suffering, money, and sweat we had invested into graduate school. We discussed our options and ideas. We were both in STEM programs, so we were eligible for a post-graduation work permit for up to two years. Our hope was to eventually find a company that would be willing to sponsor our work visas. Temi ended up being employed by a company willing to sponsor her work visa, so it worked out for her in the end. Things worked out quite differently for me.

With two different personalities, Temi and I disagreed on many things. One was her choices in terms of dating. We both had the same mindset of waiting till marriage before having sex. I would always call her out when she got carried away. She'd excitedly tell me that she was interested in a guy, but from her description, I knew their actions and words were clearly not in line with our mindset. She thought I was too strict when it came to the opposite sex, and I thought she wasn't being cautious enough.

Temi is the only friend I have with whom I have no personality traits in common, but somehow our friendship works. I can't imagine my graduate school experience without her. The type of encouragement you get from someone who's going through the same or similar experience as you is invaluable. Today, Temi and I are both financially comfortable and doing well in our respective fields. Although we live in different states now—about two hours apart—we have kept in touch. We always have plans to reconnect as soon as we both can get away from various life's commitments.

One day I was giving Temi a lecture for giving a guy the time of day when she knew he was all wrong for her. A friend of Temi's heard me over the phone and wondered who that stern sounding female was. He wanted to meet me. Temi introduced me to Kamil in November 2014. He is part Nigerian, part Ghanaian. Growing up in Nigeria, one of things that frustrated me beyond measure was how many Nigerian men think. Many of them are so entitled and are condescending towards women, but Kamil was different. His thought process and his stance on gender equality were a breath of fresh air. It gave me hope.

Kamil is the older brother I never had. I'd always wished I had an older brother. I'm not sure why. Maybe it's because I've always been in a position where I am always advising my younger siblings and steering them toward making the right choices, and I always felt that there was no one I could really turn to for advice. I still ask for his input when I need advice, and he is always ready to help.

Kamil is like me—ambitious. He is one of the very few people who gets me. We aren't the type of people to settle for less than what we believe we can achieve. Kamil and I hit it off instantly after Temi introduced us. As with people who are very alike, we butted heads a lot, but our friendship has stood the test of time. We've learned a lot from and about each other. Kamil was not a graduate student like Temi and I. He had a green card and was working full time, so that in itself was encouraging and something to aspire to.

There are times when I have almost acted recklessly, but my friends called me out on my actions and prevented me from doing things I would regret. One such friend is my darling friend, Tega. I met Tega when

I was seventeen. We were in the same class in the first year of college, and I remember not liking her very much because I thought she talked too much. At that age, I was in a fairly constant state of moodiness and generally disliked everyone.

I don't remember how Tega and I started talking but somehow, we became friends and have stayed friends for more than a decade now. Tega is my soul sister. She is not afraid to tell me the truth in love. Our friendship has gone through years of refining. If there is anyone that would look me square in the eye and call me out for doing something wrong or handling a situation poorly, it would be Tega. There are times I've had quarrels with people and told Tega about them. Rather than blindly take my side, she would point out ways in which I might not have acted kindly. That usually gives me something to think about.

She left Nigeria to move to the UK, and it was easy to keep in touch since the time difference was just one hour. When I moved to Boston, it was much harder due to the five-hour time difference, but we tried. We encourage each other and pray for each other. I am especially proud of how she maintains her values and is true to who she is.

One of my oldest friends is my brother. He is just eighteen months younger than me, so we practically grew up like twins. We have kept secrets even our parents don't know about. We have so many shared childhood memories—some painful, some hilarious. Being so close in age, we have had our share of fights over the years, but I trust my brother with my life. Many of the things I do, I do to show my siblings that they can do anything they set their minds to. I want to encourage them to think outside the box and think for themselves rather than let culture or tradition dictate their choices. We have two younger siblings, and I have watched my brother step up and be a big brother to them.

I am so proud of how ambitious my brother is and how different he thinks compared to the average Nigerian man. We don't hesitate to ask each other for advice, and we're very open with each other. I love having someone

I can tell anything to without having to sugarcoat it or beat around the bush. During the tough times I had in Boston, thinking about my siblings and the kind of example I'd set for them meant quitting wasn't an option. I wanted them to know that they could achieve whatever they set their minds to, regardless of circumstances.

Sometimes I went on walks with young ladies from church. They would walk around town "sharing their faith." It was one of those awkward religious activities I did not care for. Being the introvert that I am, I prefer meeting people on my own terms, and if conversations swung that way, I never mind talking about my faith and my belief in God. However, in the church I attended back then, it was a common practice for this group of young ladies to go out sharing their faith around Boston. Sometimes I would tag along if their faith-sharing route was on my way home. Other times I declined.

One crisp fall evening in 2015, I chose to tag along. We spotted a Black couple with a baby in a stroller ahead of us, and we stopped to talk to them. When I heard their names—Onwuegbus—I knew they were Nigerian. I introduced myself and we chatted for a few minutes. Seeing that we had something in common, the girls stepped aside to let me talk to them, expecting that I would invite them to church. I told them that we were just walking around sharing our faith, and they mentioned that they were also Christians. I exchanged numbers with them and even though I left the church not too long after that, I still maintained a friendship with the Onwuegbus. They became my family at a time when I did not have any family around. They pretty much adopted me as their younger sister. The Onwuegbus would always send me home with one food item or another, knowing that these were important to a struggling graduate student. It's been years since I finished graduate school, but we've been in touch ever since.

I got married in March of 2017. As the sort of person that likes to plan ahead, I made most of the wedding arrangements well ahead of time, including arrangements with a caterer. We had invited Nigerian and American guests, and I wanted food for both groups. I paid the caterer the deposit she requested, and everything was finalized. Or so I thought.

A week before the wedding, I decided to check in with the caterer to confirm that everything was going according to plan and to also confirm that she would be bringing the food to the reception at the agreed time. She told me that she would not be able to deliver the food before 4 p.m. We had agreed a few months earlier that she would bring the food to the reception by 3 p.m. A week before the wedding she was telling me that she would be charging an extra fee to bring the food to the venue. That was not our original agreement. I had clearly let her know where the venue's location was, and there had been no mention of any extra fees. She claimed that the fee was because the venue was in another state.

My problem with that line of reasoning was that none of the changes were news to her. When we'd agreed to work together, she'd been fully aware that the wedding was going to be in New Hampshire. Only an hour's drive from Boston on a traffic-free day. And we'd agreed on a fee to cover the entire cost of catering, including transportation. To avoid going back and forth over the issue, I texted a friend of mine who was planning to attend the wedding and was going to be driving up from Massachusetts to ask if she would be willing to pick up the food on her way. She said yes. I texted the caterer to let her know that she did not have to worry about delivering the food anymore. My friend was going to pick it up. She would be driving up around 12 p.m. to make it on time for the church ceremony.

I asked the caterer if she could prepare the food to be picked up by 12.

"No, that cannot work for me," she replied. She said she was going to the market that morning to get the ingredients for the food, and her plan was to start her cooking around 10 a.m. that morning, and she was sure she would not be done until 3 p.m.

It was a wonder my phone did not erupt into flames with the anger with which I typed my response.

How will the food be ready at 3 if you are supposed to be delivering it at 3 as we agreed to months ago? Even if the food were to be delivered by 4, 3pm is still pushing it too close. I am not willing to pay you for delivery if I have a friend willing and available to pick it up on her way to the wedding.

The caterer insisted she was not going to have the food ready by 12 and that my friend was free to pick it up at 2.

I replied again:

If she picks it up at 2 then she is going to miss the wedding ceremony at the church, I don't want her to miss my wedding because she is doing me a favor by picking up the food.

The caterer's response was that there was nothing she could do about it. I was beyond furious. I reckoned she believed I couldn't back out because the wedding was just a few days away, but I did just that. I told her I was no longer interested in working with her and that I wanted a refund of the deposit I'd given her four months earlier. I did not have a plan B.

A few days later, Tega texted me to ask how the last-minute wedding preparations were going. I told her the latest drama that had just occurred with the caterer. At the time, she wasn't sure if she would be able to make it to the wedding due to several factors, but when she heard about the problem at hand, she decided to fly to the US from the UK. She offered to take care of the meal preparation at no cost. She has her own catering business and does that as a side gig when she was not working as a pharmacist. Tega arrived in the US two days before my wedding. The next day, she, my mom, and I went grocery shopping for the ingredients she would need. The night before the wedding, Tega and two other friends, Malo and Alaba, who had flown in from Texas and New Jersey, respectively, stayed up all night cooking for my wedding.

I had had a stressful couple of days leading up to the wedding, and I was exhausted and not in the best of moods. I ended up snapping at everyone at some point and felt crappy afterward. Of course, in her own mild-mannered way, Tega pointed out that although she could understand I was under a lot of stress, my snapping at people was a jerk move. I was able to get about five hours of restless sleep the night before my wedding, but those three amazing women did not get any sleep. I would forever remember their selflessness that night. Especially Tega, who flew all the way from the UK as soon as she heard there was a need that she could fill. True, selfless friendship.

Friendship can only work if you're willing to open your heart to another person, if you're willing to trust them to have influence over your decisions. If you don't trust someone to give good, sound advice, then that person should not have any sort of influence on you. I can always be myself around my friends, and they can be themselves around me. We don't put on airs or facades around each other.

I hear stories of people whose so-called friends dare them to do dangerous or illegal things or even to commit suicide. What sort of evil friend is that? Friends are supposed to lift you up and encourage you. They are there to share your pain, cry with you, and laugh with you. Personally, I don't hesitate to cut people off if I find out that they are toxic or that they do not have my best interests at heart. There's already enough drama in the world without adding on the drama some people bring with them. That being said, every friendship, especially in its beginning stages, experiences some growing pains in the form of disagreements or personality clashes. In the beginning, people are just starting to figure out truths about each other's beliefs, backgrounds, and personalities. And if you find a friend that is "your person," it is worth investing in that friendship. If you have a friend that you cannot fully be yourself around, then there is a need to reevaluate that friendship.

Although we love our friends and want the best for them, sometimes life happens and distance sets in. Sometimes they change. I've had friends who allowed the pressures of life to make them abandon their core values. It is disappointing to see a friend go astray and make poor choices, but all we can do is advise them and hope they see the error of their ways. Maybe we can change their minds or maybe we can't. We cannot bear the consequences of their actions. They must face the music all by themselves, for there is no bad choice that does not carry a consequence. All we can do is encourage them through those consequences.

And still, there are those friends that despite all the challenges that life brings remain sure-footed, unwavering in their faith and in their assurance that they would hold on to their values no matter what. Those are the friends that inspire me and make me want to be better. There are also those friends that remind you to be grateful, those that count your blessings with you and lift you out of a depressed or discouraged mood. *Why would anyone settle for friends that leave them broke, depressed, hurt, and ashamed? Why would anyone continue to feed a friendship that leaves them feeling taken advantage of?* I don't know what that would be, but it's definitely not friendship.

If you're a follower of Christ and believe in the Scripture, then you'll understand the importance of friends as written in Proverbs. It talks about a friend that sticks closer than a brother. A friend should be one that encourages you to hold on to your convictions, not the one who tries to cause you to stray from them, especially if those convictions are rooted in the word of God. I've always had strong convictions about certain things, one of which is not having sex before marriage. At one time, all my closest friends had the same convictions too. Nothing encourages you more to stand by your convictions and beliefs than when you have close friends who hold those same beliefs. I would not have given up on my beliefs even if my friends did not share them, but it definitely helped me stick to those values especially in an environment where immorality is rampant.

I've been blessed to have friends to share the ups and downs of life with. If I were to offer any advice to a young girl who had questions about how to go about choosing friends, it would be this: find friends who encourage you, pray for you, who will be excited about your successes, and you should be the same kind of friend to others.

SEASONS OF CHANGE

I LOVED LIVING IN BOSTON. The fast pace of the city reminded me so much of Lagos, the city I grew up in. The only difference was that people avoided eye contact by all means in Boston. I've come to know that this is a common trend in New England, not just in Boston.

When I first moved to Boston, I observed as people walked around with their ears plugged with earphones. They always seemed to be looking down at the floor or at their phones as they walked. In my first few weeks of living in Boston, as I navigated the workings of the public transportation system, I needed to get directions to different bus stops and had to stop people at different times to ask for directions. I pretty much had to wave in their faces to get their attention since waiting for someone to make eye contact would have been futile. And when they did stop, I always made sure to start with "I just need directions," almost as if I was raising an imaginary white flag that read "I come in peace."

See, the expectation is that when someone stops you in a city like Boston, they are about to ask you for money. And people make a show of taking their earphones out of their ears. Gotta love city people.

In a few short months though, I changed my habits a bit and became one of those city people. Plugging my ears with my earphones, listening to music as I walked down the street to attend classes or to work. The only difference was that I did not look down. I kept my gaze up and my eyes sharp. I focused on people walking around me. There are many skills one acquires by living in a city like Lagos, where bags can be torn off your shoulders if care is not taken, or gold necklaces and wristwatches can be yanked from your neck and wrist. Vigilance while walking on the street is a skill that is still very much ingrained in me even years after leaving my homeland.

As a city girl through and through, I enjoyed the noisy bustle of Boston. I loved seeing life happen. Newbury Street, where I lived, was a wealthy neighborhood in Boston. It was a fifteen to twenty-minute walk to my university, Northeastern University, depending on how fast I walked. Rather than spend money taking the train or bus, I chose to walk to and from school daily. I can count on one hand the number of times I took the train to school in my two years of study there. Walking was more economical and reliable.

I loved summers in Boston. I'm not a nature person, but sometimes I'd stroll to the Boston Common just because I wanted to feel the heat of the scorching sun on my face and neck. I wasn't interested in watching the ducks swim in the pond or watching people feed the birds (despite clear signage telling them not to). I was there for the sun.

"Blessed heat," I'd say before letting out a big sigh, welcoming the warm embrace as I stepped out into the hot summer days. It reminded me of home. The flowers that bloom in the summer were so colorful, I had never seen anything like it.

Yet, three short months later, the weather would slowly begin to change, much to my displeasure. Although I find the turning of leaves incredibly beautiful and very fascinating since we don't experience that in Nigeria, the changeover filled me with quiet dread because I knew that winter would arrive. I looked at the fallen leaves with a bit of sadness and sighed. *Not again*. And when November rolled around, and the first signs of snow started, I sigh again but this time thinking, *here we go again*.

The winter of 2014 was my first experience with winter and snow. During the fall, I'd chatted briefly with a housemate of mine who, when she realized I had never experienced winter or snow, tried to encourage me, saying it wasn't that bad and that I would be fine as long as I bundled up.

The truth is that I hated the winter so much. Sure, snow is pretty to look at, but it can become dangerous really quick. And black ice. Why is that even a thing? I couldn't believe how humans actually live and survive in such frigid temperatures! And some people dare to say that they love the winter. I always look at winter-loving people like they have two heads.

I was ready for my first winter, though. I had my winter boots ready. I had my earmuffs, knitted gloves, leather gloves, ankle and knee-length socks, knitted hat, and knitted face mask. I wasn't there to play. I've never liked rain or cold weather, even though the coldest it gets in Lagos is about 50 degrees Fahrenheit during the Harmattan season between December and February which brings with it dusty and dry wind. I knew the Boston winter wouldn't be Harmattan weather, but I didn't know how bad it would get.

Already my first fall experience in 2014 was colder than I'd expected, so I didn't have a good feeling about the upcoming winter. Then winter came, and it was nothing I could have imagined. It was horrible. I hated every minute of it. But being the adaptable soul that I am, I just went with the flow. Even though the flow meant wearing a tank top and a long-sleeved t-shirt beneath my sweater, two leggings underneath my jeans, three pairs of socks, two pairs of gloves, earmuffs, and a winter face mask each time I stepped outside my home.

I still walked to school during the winter. I had a job on campus then and was required to show up if I was on duty, even if there was a snowstorm. I remember trudging through inches of snow at 5:30 a.m. one morning during a snowstorm as I walked to school for an early shift. I had a winter hat with a visor I could pull down, and I was bundled up to my teeth. The only uncovered parts were my eyes.

One day in winter of 2014, a few of my housemates thought it would be a great idea to go sledding downtown during a blizzard and asked if I would join them. *Sure, why not? I'm an expert at bundling up now*, I thought.

I did not yet understand the gravity of a blizzard. I soon found out that if you stayed out in the cold long enough, it could still penetrate your bones even if you were well bundled. My housemates and I bundled up and walked up Newbury Street to the Boston Common where there was a heap of snow and kids and their parents' snow sledding. It didn't look like fun to me. I've always been the type to decline activities that looked remotely dangerous, and I've always associated winter weather with danger. (I'm looking at you, black ice.) But then I figured if parents were letting their kids do it, it couldn't be that dangerous. I decided to give sledding a shot. We had makeshift sleds made from big trash can covers and something else I couldn't remember. We survived and everyone stayed safe, but I didn't really find it enjoyable.

After about half an hour frolicking in the snow, we headed back home and by then the blizzard had picked up. My fingers and toes were starting to feel numb, and I was very eager to be back indoors. As soon as we got indoors, I ran for the sink to warm my hands. That is something I now know never to try again. I turned on the hot water tap thinking the warm water would make my numb fingers feel better. Bad idea. I screamed from the sheer pain of it. For a second, I wondered if I had caused permanent nerve damage to my fingers. I ran up to my room, cupping my fingers. I took off my boots and socks and wore fresh socks, allowing my toes to warm up slowly on their own. Since I had no idea what to do with my fingers, I just sat on them until the pain went away and eventually, they warmed up and felt normal again.

By the next winter, I had completed a year of graduate school already and had met Huda, my Lebanese classmate and friend by then. We decided to go ice skating one evening, again with a blizzard in the forecast. I had never gone ice skating, so I decided to have an adventure. I guess there must be something about blizzards that tempts me to be adventurous.

We'd just put on our skating shoes when the ice storm started, but we went on the skating rink anyway. I fell on my butt a few times and had many good laughs. Eventually a young guy took pity on me and held me as he skated around. I still have pictures from that day, and I smile fondly each time I look at them. It is ironic to think that many of my fun, memorable experiences in Boston took place in the winter and involved the snow one way or another. Winter is still my least favorite season of the year.

I've experienced five more winters since that first winter and to me, each one is just as horrible as the last. You'd think that by now I would be used to it, but I'm just never ready for it. No matter how much I try to prepare myself for it psychologically ahead of time.

I recently chatted about winter sports with an older white man while at the pharmacy. He told me that the best way to not feel so miserable about the winter season is to take up a winter sport. I couldn't help my look of horror.

"What?! No way! I hate winter enough as it is. I would not step out during the winter if I did not have to," I told him.

He gave me a knowing smile and said he used to hate the winter too until he took up skiing. He said he was sure I would feel differently about the season if I tried it. I wanted to tell him that Nigerians did not partake in dangerous activities, but all I said was, "Isn't that dangerous? When I hear skiing, all I think is danger."

He said he didn't think it was as dangerous as some people thought it was and that with proper training, it was safe. I told him I would take it under advisement.

I did partake in another outdoor activity that I never thought I would ever do—hiking. In the summer of 2016, I hiked a 6,000-foot mountain with my boyfriend, and that took about three hours. That was my first time doing any sort of hiking. By the time we hiked down the mountain, my legs felt like rubber.

Shortly after I got married, I tried hiking the same mountain using a different, tougher terrain a year later. After about two hours, we were almost at the summit, but my legs wouldn't work anymore. My husband had to carry me on his back the rest of the way. I refused to hike down the mountain and rode in my sister-in-law's car instead while my husband hiked back down with his dad and his brother. The year after that I was pregnant and did not have the energy to hike up a mountain. Hiking is good exercise, but I have no desire to climb that high again.

So, I can be adventurous when I want to be. Trying these outdoor activities challenged me to get out of my comfort zone, which was really why I moved to the US. But skiing? I still don't think that's something I'm going to be trying anytime soon. But who knows? I surprise even myself sometimes.

WHAT'S IN A NAME?

ONE INTERESTING FACT ABOUT NIGERIA is that we can usually tell what tribe someone is from because of their names, except when they have English names.

Nigerian names are very meaningful, and many of them depict the circumstances of birth of the child. In the Yoruba tribe that I'm from, children born on the weekend are given a specific type of name, as well as those born during festive periods such as the New Year, those born breached, or those born with matted or locked hair. Twins and children who are born after twins also have unique names. When I hear of someone named Idowu for instance, I know he or she was born after a set of twins.

One interesting aspect of living in another country is the difficulty people seem to have with foreign names. I get it. It's not very easy learning how to pronounce names that are different from what you've known growing up. And I do try to make it easy for people. I learned a trick from my friend, Alaba. When she introduces herself, and she notices people not familiar with her name stumble on the letters, she adds, "It's like Alabama without the -ma." I thought it was funny and clever the first time I heard her say that.

I realized that the shortened form of my name also rhymed with a US state. So, when people had difficulty with the three-letter word that is the short form of my name, I add, "It's like Oregon, without the -gon." I almost always get an aha look when I say that. I've introduced myself as Ore and had people come up with Oren, and I have to say, "No, there's no 'n' after it." Somehow people come up with different words for what they hear me say, so now each time I introduce myself I have to say, "My name is Ore. O-R-E." And even with spelling it out, some people still come up with Erin. I'm always left to wonder how O-R-E ends up being Erin. My name's not that hard!

Pronunciation is one thing, but intonation is another thing entirely. In the Yoruba language, the word *ore* has about three different meanings depending on the intonation. It can mean offering, goodness, or friend. Nigerians outside my tribe rarely get the intonation right, so I don't expect a non-Nigerian to.

Luckily, I have a name with a shortened form that's not difficult to pronounce. I know some people try to modify their names to save it from being butchered by the American tongue. Interestingly, I knew of some Chinese classmates of mine in graduate school who completely changed their names to English names to make it easier for people to pronounce. Funny thing was this name was not on their documents or anything—they just picked a random English name and introduced themselves with that. I thought it was silly. They should be able to be proud of their names rather than try to make it easier for others to pronounce. As a popular African joke goes, if Americans can pronounce complex Russian names with their often-long string of letters, then they can pronounce ours too.

As interesting as Nigerian names are, for some people, the first thing they think when they hear the word Nigerian is a "prince" trying to defraud you of your hard-earned money. That's unfortunate. I feel sorry for those that have innocently fallen prey to such scams. However, financial scams are not vices unique to Nigeria.

I cannot count how many times I have received phone calls asking me to provide my social security number over the phone, so they can rectify an "issue" with my "benefits." Or calls saying that I am being prosecuted by the IRS for some error on my filed taxes and to avoid being arrested in the next twenty minutes, I have to pay a certain sum of money. Scams abound everywhere and in every country. Sometimes I imagine a world in which an imaginary hand appears from nowhere and smacks everyone who makes these sorts of calls. A few hot slaps ought to reset their brains. It's so sad to think that many of the people who fall victim to these are old people, some of whom are barely getting by with what little money they have.

Scams come in different forms. Some very obvious, and some quite subtle. I'm not the type to generalize and label a group of people or race by the actions of one member of that race. After all, the calls I get telling me I'm about to be arrested by the IRS often have men with Indian accents on the other end of the line, and American-sounding callers often call me telling me the warranty on my vehicle is expired, or that my insurance has lapsed and I have to provide private information in order for them to reverse whatever was going in. I don't believe all Indians, or all Americans are scammers. There will always be a few bad eggs in every race. And I encountered a bad egg while in graduate school.

A few years ago, while living in Boston, I had an encounter with someone who tried to play a fast one on me. Anyone who knows me knows I hate injustice. I hate people thinking they can dupe someone else and get away with it. I hate people getting away with any type of fraud. I lived in Nigeria for twenty-five years, and I saw a lot of injustice. Injustice to which there was no one to report to or ensure that justice was done. But while in the US, there was no way I was going to let anyone treat me unfairly.

One thing I appreciate about the American society as it is now, is that there are so many ways to speak up and so many different authorities to reach out to. If one tries to silence you, there's another to try. They may not always help me the way I want or need them to, but by gosh I will speak out and make my voice heard.

A friend of mine in Texas, Malo, had asked me to help her purchase some goods for sale from Primark. She'd heard that a Primark store had just opened in Boston. Since she'd made a small business out of purchasing shoes and bags from Primark each time she traveled to the UK and selling them in Nigeria when she returned, she figured she would try to do the same while she was studying in Texas. Downtown Boston wasn't far from where I lived on Newbury Street, so I did not mind going there to scout out their inventory. Malo and I agreed that I would go into the store, and I would connect with her via video call so she could see what they had in store.

Everything went as planned. Malo selected all she wanted, and I paid for them. The plan was for her to reimburse me the next day. I got a cab and went home. Malo had gotten in touch with a shipping agency in Hyde Park, Massachusetts, to ask if she could ship her goods and what the cost would be. I told her I was fine going there. I went there on my next free day with the goods and met a Nigerian man named Yemi. He looked to be in his early to mid-forties. When I told him my name, he could already tell what Nigerian tribe I was from and asked what part of Nigeria I grew up in. From his name I could tell we were from the same tribe. We chatted for a few minutes and switched to the business at hand. He weighed the bags and gave me a quote. I called Malo and she thought it was a fair price, so I paid him. He issued me a receipt and told me he would follow up with me via email once the items shipped. I thanked him and left. I got an email from him in a few days which I forwarded to Malo. The goods had shipped. All was well.

Fast-forward to about four weeks after that, and Malo asked if I was willing to do the same thing again. *Sure, why not?* We had our Primark Skype video tour, she selected the items she wanted, and I contacted the same shipping guy since everything had gone without a hitch the last time.

The second time, however, it seemed that between October and November of 2015, the shipping guy had somehow gotten it into his head that he could try to rip me off.

I went to his warehouse/office to drop off the goods like I did the last time. After weighing the bags, he gave an estimate that was almost double the cost of shipping the last set of goods. It didn't make sense because

Malo had bought fewer items and spent less money this time around. The only thing that was different was that the last time Malo had mailed me empty luggage bags to ship the shoes and bags in. This time around we were going to be using the shipping man's boxes since we had no empty bags, and he was trying to use the biggest possible boxes he could find in his warehouse. I let him know we were fine with smaller boxes since there weren't that many items to be shipped, and the items weren't all that bulky. I asked him to show me what the large boxes looked like so I could determine myself if a larger box was necessary. He claimed he did not have any in stock but was going to get more the next day. He said he would have a more exact quote after weighing the goods in the final box they would be shipped in. He said it was okay to leave the goods in his warehouse till then.

The next day Yemi called me to let me know he got the large boxes in and gave me what was, to me and Malo, an absolutely ridiculous quote. I asked him why the cost of shipping this set of goods was close to double the cost of the last set which had contained a lot more items. His only answer was that we were paying for the boxes which we had not needed to pay for before. I told him we weren't interested in paying for large boxes when the smaller ones could be used without problems. I told him we weren't interested in doing business with him anymore, and I was going to get the goods in a few days. He stated that that was fine with him.

On my next day off school (about two days or so after my last conversation with the shipping man), I informed him I would be coming to get the goods, and he told me what time to arrive. I got there and his warehouse was locked. I called him and informed him that I was at his warehouse. He told me he would give me the goods only if I paid the cost of them taking up space in his warehouse for the past two days. I was livid! I told him I was not paying a cent. I just wanted my stuff and that was it. It had started to drizzle by then and I was gradually getting soaked from the rain. I told him I would be back for my stuff when he was available, and he can tell me that to my face. His reply was, "If you come to my warehouse without my consent, you'll be trespassing, and that's how people get shot."

"Oh, so that's how it is, eh? Threatening to shoot me?" I asked him.

He hung up.

I left and went back home. I informed Malo of the latest development. She usually did not make a lot of profit from selling those items in Nigeria. She pretty much did it for the fun of running a little side business. She was in Texas, so there wasn't a lot she could do to get Yemi to release the goods. We lamented over the injustice and wished there was something we could do. She talked to a police officer on her campus and was told it was a civil issue and not a criminal one.

I began looking up the process for handling civil incidents. I read that I could sue him to court in order to have him either release the property or pay back the value of the items. I got to work at once. I showed up at the municipal court in Boston and explained the situation. I filled out the necessary paperwork and was told this would be handled by the small claims court, and that I would be informed once a date was set for the hearing.

At that time, I was babysitting for a kind Nigerian woman, Mrs. O, who was in Boston for a project that would take close to a year to complete. I loved babysitting. I was working on campus at the time, too, so from about 8 a.m. to 5 p.m., I would babysit, then rush out to catch the train in order to get to class at 5:30 p.m. Depending on the day, after class, I would walk home and then eat dinner only to walk back to school for an evening or overnight shift as a proctor for the on-campus hostels.

I narrated the story to Mrs. O., and she complained about the terrible behavior of some Nigerians who continue to give the rest of us a bad name. I told her I would let her know what the date for the hearing was as soon as I knew. I only babysat for her from Monday to Thursday each week as she traveled back home to Atlanta on Thursday afternoons. Although she was very understanding, I was hoping the hearing date would fall on a Friday to avoid having to take her baby with me to court. It did not. It fell on a week when her other children, two boys, were on summer vacation from school, so she'd brought them along with her to Boston.

So, there I was with three kids to look after. Those boys kept my heart rate up constantly as only five- and seven-year-old boys can do. Their sister was about nine months old at the time and was a very good and cooperative baby. I asked Mrs. O if it was alright to take all three kids with me to the court because I did not want to have to reschedule even if I could. I wanted to get the whole drama over with as soon as possible. She was fine with me taking them along with me.

When the day of the hearing came, I squeezed all three kids into a taxi and off we went to the court. I made sure the baby was fed before the hearing started, and I pleaded with the boys to try to be calm and quiet until we left the court. When pleading failed to work, I resorted to threatening to report them to their mom if they didn't behave. The older boy was usually very cooperative but the younger one not so much.

Shortly before the judge came in, Yemi arrived. We did not acknowledge each other's presence. A bespectacled, middle-aged, white man came in and introduced himself as the judge presiding over the case. He then introduced the case, asking us both to step forward to the plaintiff and defendant's sections. I left the boys sitting on the bench behind me while I carried the baby with me and held her on my lap as I faced the judge. During his introduction, the judge said that if we had anything else to add after our turn to speak had passed or while the other was speaking, we had to signify with a raise of a hand rather than interrupting the other person. We both swore an oath to tell nothing but the truth.

The judge then asked us to present our cases, granting me permission to go first. I narrated the story fully, making sure to include the part where Yemi had threatened to shoot me if I came to his warehouse. Then it was his turn to narrate his own version of the incident, and boy what a narration it was! Filled with omissions and lies!

Yemi stated, while under oath, that he had sent me an email telling me what the cost of shipping was going to be, and that I had failed to respond, which was what led him to decide to bill me for each day my goods spent in his warehouse. What a stupid lie especially considering that I had thought to print out every email we had ever exchanged. I had also gone in with receipts from Primark, from both shopping trips and receipts from the previous shipment he had successfully completed.

While he was spewing lies, I blurted out "What?!" The judge gave me a look as if to say *Remember what I said earlier?* I gritted my teeth and raised my hand briefly and put it back down.

Meanwhile, the boys were being noisy behind me, and the judge asked me if I could go over to "take care of my kids." He probably assumed they were all my kids. I carried the baby girl and walked over to where the boys were and through clenched teeth told them to behave, promising them we would be out soon. I went back to my assigned seat and just then the baby started to grunt, signaling that she was pooping. It was all I could do not to burst out laughing at that time. It seemed so fitting in a way.

Here I was, a young woman in her late twenties trying to fight for justice while a forty-something-year-old man was being dishonest, and a judge listened intently to both parties so he could make the best possible decision. Right then the baby was pooping freely and innocently. I sat there wishing the smell would choke the liar sitting on my far left.

The judge turned to me and asked if I had anything else to add since I'd raised my hand earlier. I said yes and told him many of the things the man had said were lies, and said I had documents to prove it. I told the judge I had a copy of the emails we'd exchanged, which clearly showed I replied to him when he sent me a quote. I turned to look at him, and I could see the surprise on his face. I gave him a look that said, *Eat that, liar!* The judge gestured for me to come forward to hand him the documents.

The judge looked at them and then asked Yemi to describe the size of the box he had been trying to sell to me. The judge took his glasses off and asked why he was trying to use that particular size for items that cost what he was looking at on the receipt. Yemi started to stutter and flipped through the stack of papers in front of him. No one knew what he was looking for in the stash.

The judge told Yemi that he believed Yemi was being unfair. Also, the judge said that Yemi didn't need that size of box to ship my goods. Thankfully, the judge said he didn't believe I owed Yemi for storage since I did not ask him to store but to ship my goods.

The judge declared that I had been treated unjustly and ordered Yemi to pay me the amount stated in my complaint form. The form had asked if I was suing for money or return of property. I had requested to be paid back the exact amount of the goods. The judge agreed that was fair and ordered him to pay it back by a specific date, and if he didn't, there would be repercussions.

I was elated! I was proud of myself for seeing this through and not getting discouraged during the entire process leading up to the hearing. I thanked the judge and gathered up the kids and left, not saying a word to Yemi.

Fast-forward to the day before the payment deadline the judge had given Yemi, and I was already looking online to see what my options were if he failed to pay. I saw that I could contact the sheriff's office and provide proof of the judgment from the small claims court and my preferred method of collecting my money, and they'd take it from there. I wrote down the number for the sheriff's office I was going to call the next day, so I was prepared.

Later that evening, I received a text from Yemi asking what address to send my check to. I rolled my eyes. Of course, he would wait till the very last minute. I replied and in a few days, I received the check. I shared the news with Malo and transferred the money to her. She insisted I take a percentage of the money for my troubles. She felt bad that I went through all that trouble just for her. I assured her seeing justice done was enough reward for me.

It felt so good to finally be living in a country where justice meant something. If we had been in Nigeria, the likelihood of Yemi getting away with his terrible and fraudulent behavior would have been very high. I would need to have better "connections" and know more highly influential people than he did to have been able to win a case like that against him.

I would have been at a disadvantage as a woman fighting against a man, being younger than him, and him being a businessman. Civil cases are seldom taken seriously in Nigeria. Best case scenario is that the police would have arrested him, kept him in custody for twenty-four hours or so, and then let him go since they couldn't really hold him longer than that without it being a criminal case. The advice would then be that we should both "sort it out between ourselves."

Many Nigerians end up privately hiring policemen, soldiers, or even thugs to scare their debtors into paying them what they owe. Nigerians can't count on the legal system—it's not very reliable and leaves many people without hope of justice.

Despite my challenges, the name Yemi isn't ruined for me. It's a common Nigerian name, and I know many Nigerians who bear the name. But this situation definitely ruined my trust in Nigerians abroad in general. You would think that Nigerians outside Nigeria would understand the struggle of leaving Nigeria for a different country and that they would be kinder, nicer, and more helpful rather than selfish and always conning their fellow Nigerians.

To me, America's name signifies hope, liberty, and justice. Justice was served in my civil case. It felt good being in a country where it didn't matter that I was young or a woman—I had the ability to call out injustice with little risk of my voice being silenced by the people who are meant to deliver justice. This isn't always the case for everyone in America, but there's certainly a better chance for justice in the US than in Nigeria.

GREEN PASTURE

SOME PEOPLE ASSUME THAT WHEN you get to America it means you have hit it big, or you now have a money tree in your yard from which you can pluck money whenever you want.

I like to think that the average human is kind enough to help a friend or relative in need if they can, and if it's within their means to do so. Not everyone can help others because they themselves might be struggling, and not many people like to admit that they're struggling. However, when people assume that you're living comfortably or in affluence, they expect you to be able to help when they ask. When you tell them you're unable to bail them out of whatever financial crisis they are in, they believe you're lying and that you just don't want to help them out of pride or selfishness. I've had a few friends and relatives do this, and I find it to be very annoying.

While I was a full-time pharmacology student in Boston, there were some points that I was juggling three jobs (two jobs plus full-time school) simultaneously. I had an on-campus job for about nine months when I realized it just wasn't cutting it. It was barely enough income to cover both my rent and my tuition. It was only enough for rent and groceries. I had to get another job, so I worked as a residential proctor. It's similar to being security personnel for the hostels. Taking that job meant I had to do overnight shifts a few times a month. The overnight and weekend shifts paid higher than the day shifts, so I usually signed up for the overnight shifts. I had classes in the evenings most weekdays, which made me unavailable to work in the evenings. Fortunately, I was able to find a job as a babysitter and did that during the daytime, four days a week.

This was my daily schedule when school was in session. Wake up at 5:30 a.m., make breakfast, pack lunch, shower, spend quiet time in prayer, leave home by 7. Take a twenty-minute stroll to the hotel where I babysat Mrs. O's beautiful, six-month-old baby. Once the baby was asleep, I would bring out my school notes and study for tests or exams. My classes started at 5:30 p.m., but Mrs. O usually returned around that time. I would leave and run to catch the train, but I was almost always late to class. And the train couldn't be counted on anyway. It was always so painful when I arrived at the train station as the doors were closing or as the train was just leaving. Then, after getting to class, I struggled to stay awake.

My classes were usually two hours long. I wasn't much of a coffee drinker, so I mostly had to rely on sheer willpower to keep my eyes open on those days. My friend, Huda and I had a few classes in common. We helped each other stay awake. We had a professor whose name rhymed with boring, as Huda liked to joke. We would always lament about how dry his lectures were. We would joke about why we chose to go to grad school instead of finding a rich prince to marry and having a dozen babies. At 8 p.m., I would begin the twenty-minute walk back home alone or with Huda. Huda lived halfway between school and where I lived, so after class, we would walk home together, chatting away for the ten minutes or so it took to get to her stop. We chatted about everything from our cultures to our plans after grad school. She is from Lebanon but lived in Sierra Leone for a bit and still has family there. It was so remarkable that even being from different countries and having different religions, we found a lot that we had in common. It was fun when I had company to walk home with, even if only halfway.

If I had an overnight shift on campus on a school night, I would get home, have dinner and then take a quick nap. My overnight shift started at 11 p.m., but I had to be in the proctor office by 10:30 p.m. to have a station assigned to me. So, usually between arriving home and having dinner, I only had time for a thirty-minute nap. Sometimes if I was too tired for dinner, I'd head right to bed for about an hour of sleep in. I would wake up at 10 p.m. and prepare some Nescafé to take along for my shift. Although I am not a coffee drinker, it came in useful sometimes when I needed to stay awake. Many times, I wanted to study during my night shifts, especially during the exam periods. Unfortunately, the coffee did not always work. Probably because I cannot stand bitter coffee, so I would always put in a generous amount of milk and sugar to mask the bitter taste. Sometimes I would put in less milk and grimace all through drinking it down, but at least it kept me awake all night.

If the next day was a babysitting day, I would walk home after my shift ended at 6 a.m., get in the shower, grab breakfast, and start my morning walk to babysit. Those were usually tough days because I would have to babysit for about nine hours on zero sleep. And if I had a class that evening, it made a tough day even tougher. By the time 5:30 p.m. rolled around, I was usually pretty sluggish physically and mentally, but I had to attend classes. Some professors would pass out attendance sheets to record attendance, and I didn't want any issues. Even though all I wanted to do was go home and fall into bed, I would hurry to catch the train and make it to class. By the time I would get home at 8 p.m., I was ready to collapse for a week. On nights like that, I did not even bother with dinner. All I wanted was sleep, so I would take a quick shower and very soon afterward would be out like a light.

After about six months of that, I had been able to save enough to start applying to get a foreign pharmacist graduate equivalency certificate. That meant I had to take a couple of exams. The application to take the exam was $1,200 at the time, and the TOEFL exam (an English proficiency exam) was about $180. I had to study for the exam since I had not practiced pharmacy in about two years since leaving Nigeria. I needed a refresher on pharmaceutical calculations and the dreaded pharmaceutical chemistry. I was taking pharmacology courses in grad school, so that helped with the pharmacology aspect of it. I had to study for the pharmacy exam alongside my school exams and continuing work. I was hoping to take the foreign pharmacist graduate exam that April even though it coincided with the end of my final semester at Northeastern. There were only two times each year where you could sit for that exam—April and November. If I did not take it in April, I had to wait till November. But I was finishing grad school in May and did not want to wait. I was hoping to have a job after graduate school.

I was under so much stress managing graduate school and my jobs that I almost flunked one of my courses. I received an email from the program coordinator, who also happened to be one of my professors, inviting me to come discuss my latest grades. I went to see him in his office that day, and he had this caring paternal look on his face that almost made me cry. *Girl, you better pull yourself together!* I scolded myself.

I'd never had a professor call me to their office before over my grades, and I had never failed at any course in all my years of schooling. I felt so anxious in his office. He started by saying I had been doing so well since I started the program and always had good grades, but one of the grades on my last midterm exams was bad. It was a course he taught, so he handed me my midterm exam sheet together with the answer key and asked me to go through both just in case something wasn't right. I looked at my answers and sure enough, I had more wrong answers than right answers. He looked at me gently and asked if everything was alright.

That really made me want to bawl like a baby. *No, everything is not alright. Nothing is alright. I am stressed out of my mind. I am having trouble keeping up with my tuition, and I don't have enough time and energy to study. And your exam questions are too difficult!* I managed a smile and nodded. "Yes, everything is alright, sir. I'm just a little stressed by a few things going on in my life right now. I will make sure I put extra effort into the finals."

He asked if I was keeping an eye on my cumulative GPA. I told him no. A hold had been placed on my student account because I had not paid my latest tuition installment, so I was unable to view my grades online. He logged in with his administrative privilege and said he couldn't show me my grades, but he couldn't stop me if I wanted to turn his laptop around and take a peek at my grades. I got the hint, so I turned his laptop around and was able to see my GPA for the first time in a while. He reassured me that my cumulative GPA was still very good and that I just had to make sure I scored at least a C+ on the final exam to pass the course and graduate. Otherwise, I had to retake the course. I thanked him and left.

I couldn't sleep that night. I could barely keep up with my tuition payments as it was, *how would I be able to keep up with the cost of enrolling to retake a course I failed?* I couldn't afford it. All my sweat, all my time, and all my money would all be wasted if I failed. I could not let that happen. I decided to assign more time to the problematic course. Fortunately, even though there was still a hold on my student account by the financial department, I was still able to attend classes and take exams. I just did not have access to view my grades. Unfortunately, to register for the following semester, my final semester, I had to pay off all outstanding debt. I did not have the money to do that.

I had to come up with $19,000 to enroll for my final semester which in itself would cost another $11,000, but I decided to worry about that later. Being an international student is a very peculiar position to be in. We pay much higher tuition rates than both local and out-of-state students, yet we are not legally allowed to work off-campus until the second semester and then only if we have a 2.5 GPA or higher. Even then, the off-campus job has to be related to our course of study. The schools earn a lot of money from us, but we are not truly free to work off-campus to recoup that money. It is a tricky situation. If domestic students were allowed to and are able to work while in school, why couldn't we? I could not relate pharmacology to babysitting even if I tried. *Um, sir, actually my babysitting job allows me to study how drugs and babies relate in terms of chemical structure?* No.

I'd been able to save some money from my babysitting gig, but it was nowhere near $19,000. Between September 2014 when I started the program to January 2016, I had already paid about $35,000 in tuition fees and other school-related expenses. I don't know how I did it, but somehow I did. From all my savings from home and my parents' contribution. With the naira currency crashing steadily day after day, whatever sum of money my parents would send would not amount to a lot. Not that they had anything more to give me. They reminded me that they had three other children to support, so they could not send me all their life savings just because I wanted to pursue graduate studies. My mom had taken pity on me and loaned me close to $7,000 the previous semester to pay off the tuition debt I had then. And although he had previously promised to give me some money, my dad had said to me, "I can't give you any more money. If things are not working out for you over there, you can come back to your country."

That statement sparked a flurry of thoughts. *Come back to where? I am not going back! What would I be returning to? I had spent all my life's savings and investments up to this point. What was there to go back to anyway? I've seen how a civilized nation works, and I'm not returning to the mess over there without a fight.*

With that, I marched to my nearest Citibank branch and asked about their personal loan options. As an international student, I did not qualify for federal or private student loans without a cosigner. The bank official asked what I wanted the loan for, and I just said, "School-related expenses." I had heard from someone before that if you said it was for school tuition, they either would not give you the loan, or they would charge you exorbitant interest rates. I was not sure how true that was, but I was not taking any chances. I was approved for a $5,000 loan on the spot.

I could not believe it. I'm not sure what trends they saw in my account that made them believe I was creditworthy, but I thanked them and walked out as fast as I could before they could change their minds. Although now that I think about it, that was the account I used for wiring funds from my Nigerian bank for my tuition payments. So, they probably saw that as a good sign. So $5,000 down, $14,000 to go.

Laura was one of the ladies I lived with at Bethany House (the Urban Ministry house). She got a position as one of the resident coordinators shortly after I moved in, so she was able to move into a fairly spacious apartment in the basement of the house. I, along with other friends, helped her move. I love Laura. We spent many hours talking about our hopes and plans for the future, our values and ideals, and what an ideal future husband looked like for us in terms of spiritual qualities. We also spent time talking about our faith and prayed about our challenges and the difficult decisions we had to make. There we were, an African girl very far away from home and a white American girl a little closer to home, but still far away from her hometown in Montana, bonding over shared values and our faith in God, pouring our hearts out to each other without judgment.

Nearly every other day, Laura would invite me downstairs to her apartment for crepes and/or to chat about a new project she was working on. She would always ask how she could pray for me after every tête-à-tête, and we would both pray for each other. I happened to be in her apartment one day when she asked what I'd been up to lately. I shared my tuition issue with her and asked her to pray for God to make a way. She looked at me and said, "I have $3,000 saved. I can loan it to you."

I was stunned. "Are you sure?" I asked. I'm not one to ask people if they are sure if they make any type of offer. If they say they will do something, I assume they mean it until I'm proven wrong. And when I make an offer and people ask if I'm sure, my thought is *yes, I am sure*. I wouldn't offer if I wasn't sure. But Laura's offer was so unexpected that I had to ask.

She reassured me and said that she had recently felt it laid on her heart to set some money aside in savings, and she did not know why but had done it anyway. I assured her I would pay her back in three months. I had done the math and figured my babysitting job would help me save enough to pay her back by then. My school job covered my rent, and the babysitting job covered everything else. It was about a week left to the deadline to register for classes, and I had $11,000 left to raise. I heard about a credit union through Temi so I contacted them. They were only able to give me a loan of $1,500. My friend, Malo, in Texas was able to loan me $600, and I had $1,500 in my savings. My dad came through and was able to give me a portion of the amount he'd promised me for my tuition about a year prior, and my mom helped to cover the rest. I like to believe my parents had a lot of faith in me and believed I was going to make it in the end, so they tried their best to help me despite their own struggles.

By some crazy miracle and the help of friends and my parents, I was able to make up the full $19,000 by the week of the deadline. I paid my outstanding balance and was able to register for courses for my final semester. About two weeks later I was able to pay Malo back, and I made very sure that I kept my word to Laura and paid her back in full within three months. She did not have to give me her savings, yet she did it so willingly and happily. Sure, we were friends and we had a good idea about each other's character. But still, loaning such an amount of money to anyone is pretty risky. Money has caused serious rifts between friends and even family members. Laura took a big risk on me, and I made sure she did not regret it. I would forever be indebted to her over that one act of kindness even though I've long since paid back the loan. I truly don't know what would have happened if she had not been able to help.

A few weeks later, a new hold was put on my student account because I did not meet the deadline to pay the first installment for the current semester. I wasn't too bothered. I was able to attend classes, take exams, and graduate. I figured I would take care of that after I started a professional job following graduation.

I have always believed that if you dwell long enough on the cons of doing something that could be worthwhile, you'll get discouraged and not muster the courage to do it. I had an idea of what the tuition for graduate school would be before I left Nigeria, but I chose not to dwell on the fact that at that time, I could only afford two semesters worth of tuition. I did not let it discourage me from pursuing a path I felt led to pursue. I believed that God would make a way and things would work out in my favor. Looking back now, completely debt-free, I can see that God did make a way, and everything did work out in my favor.

My American journey, especially graduate school, has tested my faith, tested my patience, and tested my resolve. It's been one of tears, prayer, learning, adventure, incredible experiences, amazing friendships, hope, and faith. I would not be where I am today if I had not taken a leap of faith despite all the cons I could see.

On April 1, 2016, I took the foreign pharmacist equivalency exam. After a nerve-racking, four-week wait, one day before graduation, I found out that I passed. I had also passed all my courses in school and even managed to get a B in the course I'd done poorly in during midterms. I was happy to finally be finished! By August, I got a job as a pharmacy intern to get the minimum hours required to qualify for the Pharmacy Board exam. It was the next step to becoming a US pharmacist.

About six months after graduate school, a relative of mine was demanding money from me. When I told them I did not have it, they proceeded to point out that I had a car, I was renting an apartment, and I was buying clothes. They wondered how I could say that I did not have money to give them.

Not a lot gets to me. People could say whatever they wanted about me, and it wouldn't bother me. I might get a little irritated if they went too far. Those words, though. Those words pierced my soul and hurt deeply, especially coming from a close relative who was privy to my struggles early on. I had a page worth of an email reply, but I deleted it and chose not to respond.

What I wanted to say was that yes, I had a car which I had to get because my internship was in another state, so it was either spend a lot of money on a two-hour bus ride every day to work and another two-hour ride back home, do an eighteen-hour walking trek to work each day, or get a car. A car was not a luxury for me at that time. It was a necessity.

I had used public transportation to attend the job interview for that particular internship position since I did not have a car at the time. I remember having to take a train and then a bus. And that day there had been some drama at the bus station, causing a delay. After about thirty minutes of delay, I had to email to let the HR officer know that I would be late. Great way to make a first impression. I had given more than enough time to factor in minor delays, but nothing prepares you for an hour-long delay. I remember having to reschedule that interview because we were told that the bus had some mechanical issues and would take a few hours to repair. Thankfully they were flexible in rescheduling. But I couldn't imagine going through that daily transportation challenge for the next ten months of internship.

I did not need a car to live and attend school in Boston since the transport system there was pretty efficient. It'd never occurred to me to get one. When having one became a necessity, I got the cheapest car I could afford. I wasn't driving a Range Rover or a fancy, flashy car, so I'm not sure why my relative felt having a car was synonymous with affluence. I clearly remember paying $1,900 for my 2001 Toyota Avalon, which drained my savings at the time. But it served me well and faithfully for two years.

Some international students go on shopping sprees after arriving in America, but I took a different approach. I remember packing my luggage for my trip to America two years earlier. My mom had come into my room and asked why I was packing up nearly all the clothes that I owned. I told her I wasn't planning on buying any clothes in the near future since I was planning to be very careful with my money when I got to America. My clothes probably took up two of the four bags I lugged around the airport and down the streets during my journey. My mom and I had gone shopping for winter jackets before I left Nigeria. Nigeria is generally hot all year round. It never gets cold enough to need a winter jacket. So it isn't something one will easily find in stores. But my mom knew of a place that might have them. It was a market where used clothes were sold. Usually those that had been imported from Western countries. We found some winter jackets there and settled on two that looked like they would hold up well in the winter. I didn't think to get winter shoes because, having no prior experience with snow, I didn't know what to expect or prepare for. My knowledge of America at that time was that it was cold. I didn't have a frame of reference for just how cold it got.

Also, at Bethany House, we had a system where we would put items that we no longer wanted for someone else to pick up if they were interested. We called it "the free table." Anything on the free table was up for grabs. People would put lamps, bags, shoes, clothes, books, and all sorts of things on there. The rule was that whatever was put on the free table had to be in good condition. No ripped clothes or damaged items. There was the trash for all that.

At one point, I became a staff member at the house and I, with other staff members, had to clean up the free table because there ended up being so much stuff that we had to bag them up and send them out to the Salvation Army. Throughout my stay in Bethany House, I was able to snag a few good finds on the free table. I was baffled at how people could buy clothes, wear them a few times and not want it anymore. I have clothes I've worn since I graduated from college. And I still wear them. I wouldn't buy clothes I don't like in the first place. When I buy something for myself, then I fully intend to use my money's worth out of it.

After experiencing the chill of the fall, I swapped a few of the short-sleeved t-shirts I owned for some long-sleeved ones I found on the free table. It's always a pain trying to buy items of clothing that fit me well since I'm on the thin side, but luckily, I found some in extra small. I also found some sweaters that I ended up grabbing. When one of my housemates recommended I get snow boots because I'd need them in the winter, I took a trip to Burlington Coat Factory to get some since that seemed like the best place to find good quality boots within my budget (thanks, Google!). I bought two pairs—a black and a brown pair. I used those boots for four winters until they began to show wear and tear and only then did I retire them. Even when I could afford to splurge on boots, I was somewhat attached to those pairs. They were the first winter boots I bought for my first winter in Boston. I couldn't bring myself to throw them away, so I donated them. Their soles were still pretty solid and holding up very well, but some parts of the leather were starting to peel off. I figured it was time to let them go. Hopefully, someone who could not afford winter shoes would get them, and they would serve them well.

The first time I actually shopped for clothes in America was in the summer of 2016, nearly two years after I arrived. I remember taking a stroll to Forever 21 down the block from the house and buying two pairs of leggings—a black and a blue pair. I wasn't going around wearing designer clothes. I was living strictly within budget. I dined out less than ten times in the three years I lived in Boston because I preferred to cook my own meals, and it was cheaper too.

So, someone using such an argument as *well you bought clothes, got an apartment, and bought a car* as a reason why I had no right to say no to giving them money was absolutely unfair. I had quite the epistle typed up to send back as a reply to my relative, but I decided it was not worth it. Anyone who knows me knows how difficult it is to hold my tongue in certain situations, especially when someone is being unfair. But even I have been known to take the higher road on occasion.

I graduated with my master's degree in May 2016. Two weeks before that, my mom and my brother arrived in Boston. It was so great to see them again after two years. When we left the airport, my mom was shocked by the cold weather. I think that was the point when I actually became *Americanized* because I said, "This? It's not even that cold." Those were brave words coming from someone who thought it was always cold in New England and that summer was the only tolerable weather.

I was so happy to see them and to show them a small part of Boston. We strolled through the area near my house, and I took my mom shopping. Shortly after arriving, my mom asked if she could get Nigerian food. I told her I hadn't had time to cook since I'd been busy with exams, but I could take her somewhere to have a burger in the meantime. She was not a fan of burgers, but she accepted my offer.

Since Bethany House only housed girls, I couldn't have my brother stay with me, so I had my friend, Kamil, house him for a few days. I finally found some time to take my mom to the only Nigerian restaurant in Boston. She was happy to finally eat some Nigerian food after being away from Nigeria for only two weeks. After, we went grocery shopping so she could make her own Nigerian food at the house.

My dad was unable to make it for my graduation. When my grandmother and aunty who lived in Florida heard about it, they insisted on being invited to "represent" him at my graduation. This was the same aunty I had reached out to a few months earlier when I was struggling to make up my tuition payment. I had asked if she was able to loan me some money or cosign a loan for me, if possible. I assured her I was going to pay her back if she loaned me the money. She told me that she was unable to because she had other family responsibilities. She is unmarried and has no children and has worked as a doctor in the US for decades, so I had assumed she was in a position to lend me some money. I did not take any offense at her refusal to help. I hadn't been expecting a positive response when I had asked. I had not wanted to ask, but I figured I might as well try every possible option.

When my mom found out I had asked my aunty for money for my tuition she was pissed. "You shouldn't have asked her!" she yelled.

"Well I had no other choice. I wanted to try all my options before going to the bank for a loan," I replied.

To date my mom still gets a little irritated when she remembers that I had asked my aunt for money. She believes that my aunt and grandmother are not nice people. And in all the years I've known them, I haven't seen otherwise.

I could only get two tickets for guests to attend my graduation ceremony, and of course those tickets automatically belonged to my brother and my mom. They were the only guests I cared about having at my ceremony. I told my aunty and my grandmother that I was only able to get two tickets for my brother and my mother. My aunty replied with a text: "If I were you, I would at least make sure one ticket goes to your grandmother." I was so irritated. *If I were going to choose between my grandma and my brother, who does she think I would choose? A grandmother I'm not even close to? A grandmother who mistreated us when we were kids?*

Since I was doing alright by myself at that point, my aunty and grandmother both wanted to act like they were a part of it from the beginning and supported me in any way. Obviously, I couldn't tell them that because it would have been considered extremely rude in Yoruba culture. Still, I did not for a minute consider getting them tickets to graduation. I heard some students were selling their tickets. Mostly international students who had family far away, who for some reason or another could not attend the ceremony. I reached out to someone who was selling hers for $100 apiece. *Nope.* Not gonna pay that kind of money for people I was not even interested in having at my graduation celebration.

Later I found that the school was offering free tickets for satellite viewing of the ceremony, which was still on campus. That was perfect. My family would be in the main auditorium while my aunty and my grandmother could view it from the satellite location. I told my aunty and grandmother that I was able to secure tickets for them. Thankfully, they finally got off my back. That was two days before the ceremony, but apparently it wasn't too last-minute for them since they were still able to get a flight and make it on time to the ceremony. Something tells me that they would still have come regardless of whether I had tickets for them or not. Or maybe they were so sure that I would have given my brother's ticket to one of them. One thing that grated on my nerves was that not once did my aunty ask how I was able to come up with the money for my tuition. She acted like that episode never happened. I guess she figured if I was graduating, then I had found a way to sort things out.

The ceremony went well. I was very proud of myself and my accomplishments. I had worked very hard for them. Having my foreign pharmacist certificate was the first step in the series of steps of starting my pharmacy career in the US, so I was feeling proud of myself for all the sweat and money I'd invested. I could almost ignore the presence of my other relatives. We all went out for a celebratory dinner afterward, with other friends joining. That night I received a gold necklace as a graduation present from a friend who became my boyfriend, then my husband. I still have that necklace on today.

America always seems like greener pasture to many people in a less-developed country, and in many ways it is. But that does not in any way mean it is an easy road. There is still the need to put in the work, avoid the temptation to compare oneself with others, and ensure one lives within one's means. It is also important to avoid getting sucked in into the credit society that America is. That will help keep you out of debt. Again, living within one's means—sometimes below—is a good way to avoid the need to take on unnecessary credit and debt. The green pasture can turn sour quickly when people remove their focus from the primary aim of making their lives and their family's lives better to instead get distracted by a frivolous lifestyle and keeping up with the Joneses.

OYINBO

ONE OF THE JOYS OF being married to someone from a different country and culture is that I get to share a lot about my culture with him, and in doing so, I get to learn things about my culture I never cared to know about before.

There is a lot about my culture that I do not care for. As a teenager, I wanted to escape it. I hated having to kneel on the floor to greet elders. I hated having to curtsy to greet adults especially if they were around my parents' age. I hated having to hold my tongue when someone older was being unfair to me or somebody else. This was an expectation from the younger person; it was considered rude to confront older people, especially if they were in a position of authority such as a teacher, an employer, or a parent.

Respect is a very big deal in Yoruba culture, and it takes on so many forms. It's in the way we address and greet older adults, and it's in our posture when we are being addressed by an older adult. To greet an older adult, females are expected to kneel with their knees touching the ground—it's not enough for the knees to just hover above the floor. Males, on the other hand, are expected to lay prostrate on the ground. Depending on the age of said adult, a female can get away with either a quick, sharp dip of the knees or a low curtsy in place of a full knees-to-ground kiss, and a male can do a quick or low bow. This usually involves a rough estimate of the adult's age. If they look to be about our parents' age, then oftentimes we can get away with the informal, sharp knee dip and quick bow. If they are older than our parents, then we must go all out with both knees touching the ground and full prostration. It's one aspect of my culture I have never understood or agreed with. I get kneeling and prostration when one is greeting a king or a queen, but why do that for one's parents or relatives? I mean I could hate your guts and wish you dead and still kneel in greeting. That does not show that I respect you. Yorubas do not care. They don't care if you do it with an attitude or not, they just want you to do it.

A roughly ten-year age gap or more usually means we must address the person as *aunty* or *uncle*. For someone older than your parents, such as your parents' uncles and aunts, they are not to be referred to as aunties or uncles but as mommies and daddies. God forbid you call them by their first names! There will be a family meeting to determine your fate if that ever happens. We don't usually address our bosses by their first names either. We call them either sir or madam. I must admit, addressing my managers and bosses in America by their first names, and not always saying "yes, ma'am" and "yes, sir" to everyone older than me took some getting used to. The first name part I have managed to get used to. Dropping the "yes, ma'am" and "yes, sir" are still work in progress. It's such a part of me that it's a hard habit to break—not that it's a bad habit or anything.

As a fresh college graduate just entering into the workforce in Nigeria, I used to always wonder why employees would go crazy when they were around their bosses. They seemed to lose sense of who they were. I had two encounters with two different bosses I had, and I left both situations satisfied that I remained true to myself and refused to be intimidated.

One of these encounters was while I was a pharmacy intern at a teaching hospital in Lagos, only one month after graduating. I was working in one of the outpatient departments one day when I accidentally gave a patient some medications meant for someone else. The pharmacists pretty much left the interns to do the work and answered any questions we had. They stepped in only when there was a crowd of people and they saw a need for extra sets of hands. The department head, a woman in her sixties at the time, arrived at work just then, and everyone around her was curtsying. I greeted her without curtsying since I did not see the need for curtsying in a formal setting like a place of work. I don't know why she chose to single me out that morning, but she came over to me and yelled at me for having a disorganized work surface, saying that was a good way to make an error.

Just then we realized I had made an error and she went ahead to yell some more. There wasn't much I could do or say in response, so I just stared at her. She seemed to take offense at that and said I would be solely responsible for tracking down the patient and retrieving the medications from them. I said I would try. I really did not understand the source of her anger. She seemed to get more annoyed as I stood there quietly. In my head I was trying to figure out how to fix the mistake, how to get the patient's number, and hoping they hadn't gone too far. I was sorry that I had made an error that could put someone in danger, but I was too occupied to pay attention to the fact that she was expecting me to be sorry that I had made her upset. Her feelings were the least important things to me at the time. She turned and walked into her office.

A few of the pharmacists came to me and advised that I had to go to her office to apologize to her. I refused to do so. If she chose to be angry, that was on her. I wasn't her child that she could scold on a whim. I had not done anything to deserve being picked on. Yes, I had made an error, but I was an intern. I was there to learn how not to make errors as a pharmacist. It should have been a learning moment rather than a bashing moment with name-calling. I would have apologized for my error if she had given me space to talk in between yelling. I guess I was expected to interrupt her to apologize, and I should have looked contrite. She'd mentioned while yelling that I did not look sorry enough for my mistake. *Can't I feel sorry for making a mistake without crying or looking morose?* Her yelling had been a way to intimidate me, to make me feel small. Even at the age of twenty-two, I didn't let anyone intimidate me. I always assume CEOs, managers or heads of departments worked hard to get to where they are, and I always respect them for it. But I refuse to treat them like demigods. They don't have two heads. I'm not sure why I need to curtsy or hang my head in deference with my hands behind my back every second I'm in their presence. They are humans just like me, and I don't do eye-service.

Fast-forward to three years later, when I worked as a pharmacist in one of the biggest retail chains in Lagos. A new store had just opened, and a few of us were pulled from other stores to help start it off. We sometimes had time to goof around since we did not have a lot of customers in the beginning. One day, while the morning dragged on slowly, I walked upstairs to chat with the makeup artist who was a resident in the makeup store above the pharmacy. I allowed her to talk me into a free makeover. I was not used to wearing makeup back then. My idea of makeup was using eyeliner and lipstick. If I were feeling extra fancy, I would apply some eyeshadow. I didn't use foundation or setting powder and all that. Those were beyond my expertise.

So, I had no idea that the foundation and powder that the makeup artist was putting on my face would soon be sitting on my white pharmacist coat. Coincidentally, that was the same day the CEO chose to visit the new store. She took a look at my collar and asked why I was wearing a dirty coat to work. At the time, I was confused since I had not yet realized the havoc the makeup had wreaked on my collar. I had washed and ironed my coat the day before and hadn't been rolling around on the ground, so I was very sure my coat was clean. I told her I was wearing a clean coat and she got angry, accusing me of lying. She turned to another staff member that had come visiting with her, and pointing to my coat she asked, "Does that look like a clean coat to you?"

That was when I looked down at my collar and saw what she was seeing. I opened my mouth to explain that it was makeup and to apologize, but I felt someone nudge me to be quiet instead of trying to speak. Not that the CEO was going to listen to what I had to say, anyway—she preferred to go on yelling about how dishonest I was being.

I don't get embarrassed easily. When bosses choose to call me out in front of an audience, I respond the same way I would if they were chewing me out in private: quietly and looking them in the eye. Oh, did the CEO feel even more triggered that I was not cowering in shame. My instinct is always to defend myself regardless of the consequences. The way I saw it, I would rather be scolded for exactly what I did rather than over an assumption or some perceived offense. I would have preferred to have been yelled at for going upstairs to get my makeup done during work hours since that was actually the wrong thing to do, rather than for being dishonest, since I had been telling the truth.

I don't like the kinds of systems that are in place in nearly all workplaces in Nigeria where a CEO or manager can yell at employees without giving them the opportunity to explain themselves, and the employees are just expected to swallow insults all in the name of respecting their bosses. What happened to respect for the employees? Last time I checked, employees were humans too. Unlike in the US, managers and CEOs are not addressed by their first names in Nigeria, and I believe that's part of the divide between employees and their bosses.

Pretty much the only people we call by first names are younger siblings, people in your age group, and co-workers. Even with siblings and co-workers, it can vary. If the co-worker is elderly, then as Yorubas, usually we would add mommy or daddy to their first names while addressing them. Different Yoruba families have different preferences for what they teach their children to call their older siblings. In my family, my younger siblings do not address me by my first name. My first brother is just eighteen months younger than me, so he gets to call me by my first name. Our two younger siblings have always addressed us as sister __ and brother __ for as long as they could speak. My dad was responsible for the rule. Of course, as they grew older now, they have shortened it to sis and bro.

With the emphasis the Yoruba culture places on respect, Yorubas expect respect from everyone, and they get easily offended if they feel they're not getting the respect they deserve. This has caused a lot of friction between Yoruba people and other tribes who don't share the same view on physical and verbal display of respect. No culture or tribe is perfect. In embracing the beautiful parts of one's culture, sometimes one also must tolerate the annoying aspects as well.

Through discussions with my husband about my culture, I've come to appreciate certain aspects of my culture even as some have left me annoyed.

One of the beautiful parts of Nigerian culture is the traditional weddings different tribes have. I've attended only a handful of traditional weddings. In some of them, I was too young to understand what was going on, and when I was older, I was not interested in attending social events since I did not enjoy being around too many people at a time. A Yoruba traditional wedding is not much different from any other Yoruba party. There is loud music, food, lots of dancing, and somewhat annoying MCs.

In Nigeria, a couple does at least two types of weddings. A court wedding and a traditional wedding. Some go ahead to have a third—a church wedding for Christians and a Muslim wedding for Muslims. We had a church wedding in New Hampshire and six months later, after barely recovering from the expense and stress of planning a wedding, we traveled to Nigeria for a Yoruba traditional wedding.

I was glad to be back in Nigeria, if only to experience the blessed heat once again. It was winter weather in New Hampshire when we left for Nigeria, so it felt so good to not have to bundle up to go outside.

Being in Nigeria with my white American husband was quite an experience. It was very much like walking around with a neon sign on my forehead. Everywhere we went, people would yell *oyinbo*, Nigerian slang for a white person. We went with my mom to one of the busiest markets in Lagos and watched my mom drive hard bargains as is the usual practice in Nigerian markets. I was so proud of my husband. He was such a good sport about being the only white person around and was happy to jump in on some of the adventures Lagos had to offer. He shook hands with one of the market helpers whose job was helping customers carry heavy loads to their vehicles for a fee. Sometimes they carried these heavy loads on their heads, necks, or shoulders. Although it was just a handshake, I could tell it made the market helper feel good to be appreciated for his hard work in an environment where he probably had orders screamed at him and was looked down upon. A group of men who had witnessed the handshake had remarked on how nice of a gesture it was and how happy they were to see a foreigner showing appreciation for what looked like and was, indeed, very hard work.

Later that day, I took him on a quick shopping trip to a street market, and we had a hard time finding transportation back to the hotel. We heard that there was heavy traffic ahead, so we hopped on a motorcycle. The motorcycle had no helmets which was not strange to me. We held on for dear life as the driver weaved in and out of traffic like a maniac, occasionally driving on the wrong side of the road to bypass the terrible traffic. Before we'd gotten on, he'd told us that policemen did not like it when motorcycles went beyond a certain point on our destination street, but he was willing to risk it for a higher fare. We got to a stoplight—one of the few that actually work in Ikeja—and there was a police stand there. We came to a stop, and the policemen seemed interested in the motorcycle with a white man on it. They commended his sense of adventure and shook hands with him, congratulating us when they heard we were newlyweds. They told him to take care of their "sister" (me) and gave the motorcycle driver a scolding for having gone beyond the point motorcycles were allowed. The light turned green, and we were on our way again. My husband thought that was one of the coolest experiences he'd had. I have taken motorcycle rides so many times that for me it was normal. They tend to be more reckless than bus drivers, and I've had to smack one on his back for driving so recklessly he almost caused an accident. Sometimes I wonder how I survived such a chaotic city.

Our traditional wedding was scheduled for the weekend after our arrival, and my mom was very busy making final preparations while I took my husband sightseeing. My husband's parents and his brother were able to make the trip, thankfully. They had had an unpleasant experience obtaining visas with the Nigerian embassy in the US, so their previously booked flight had changed.

It was good to share a piece of my homeland with my husband and his family. I had an enjoyable time playing tour guide, and I got to learn about a few sights I was unfamiliar with in Lagos even though I had lived there for all my life before leaving for the US.

I find my husband's description of our visit to Nigeria very intriguing.

Tuesday

When our plane touched down, some people exclaimed "Thank you, God," and others started clapping. Trying to fit in, I started clapping along, much to Ore's ire. Nothing irritates her quite like pointless clapping.

Then half the plane jumped up to grab their bags, unaware that we still had to taxi for a while. "Please remain seated" shouted the flight attendant over the radio, but it was too late. They had to go down the aisle and make each person sit down, offending a few in the process.

We left the plane and were immediately in a new environment. New and different to an extent I hadn't experienced in years. The international terminal's walkway was full of Nigerians waiting for their departing flights. It seemed like the walkway was the only place they could wait for their flights. (Note: This was disputed by Ore.)

Soon we reached the first passport inspection point. Ore left for the Nigerian passport line, and I found myself alone with the guards. They took my passport and vaccination card and looked them over. "Harmy? Your name is Harmy?" They asked, quite amused by what they saw. "You must be very strong if that is your name!" I nodded politely and smiled, too nervous to think of a witty response. They ushered me into a slow-moving line and gave me an immigration card to fill out.

The line moved slowly, and I was the fourth from the back. Eventually, they pulled out one guy behind me for faster service since he had a resident card. Then they accelerated a family of three behind me who didn't have a card, leaving me in last place.

When I finally got to the passport desk, a stern woman looked at my passport picture and then at me several times. Knowing that I looked unrecognizable in my picture from five years ago, I smiled and told her I had lost weight, trimmed my beard, and shaved my head. She looked a couple more times and then started calling for her supervisor. "Is this him?" she asked. He looked a few times and then agreed that it was me.

I went to the next desk and then through to baggage claim. There I met up with Ore, and we passed by the secondary inspection checkpoint without an issue and finally exited to the terminal.

No sign of anyone we knew in the arrival terminal. So, there we waited. A few guys came up to us to offer rides, but only one bothered to keep standing there after we turned him down. Ore's plan was to put her old SIM card in her phone and give her mom a call that way. After changing the SIM in a delicate operation, we learned that it no longer worked. The driver who was still eavesdropping offered to let her use his phone to call her mom, for a small fee. She took him up on it, but there was no answer.

Ore decided we should walk out to the curb and see if her mom was outside. As we walked out, there was a wall of taxi drivers and other miscellaneous men walking around, all of them happy to see us. We walked down the curb a bit and didn't see Ore's mom. We decided to stand by the wall and wait, growing increasingly worried by the minute.

Then, out of the blue, Ore's mother appeared and greeted us. At that point, I breathed a huge sigh of relief. Few men have ever been so happy to see their mother-in-law.

Ore's mother led us down the walkway a bit to a bus stop/taxi drop-off point. She had a friend with her, and she sent him to fetch our cab. While we waited, I got to see a scrum of people trying to force their way onto a bus. It was quite the full-contact affair.

Eventually, our point person came back with the cab driver, and we walked to the parking garage together. We took some time to clarify to our driver which hotel we were staying at, thankfully I had remembered the neighborhood name and could confirm it for him. We were parked near a couple of minibuses full of foreigners. Looking at their host's vest, I was able to piece together that they were on a pilgrimage of sorts to T.B. Joshua's church in Lagos. It's a very odd organization, by any country's standards.

We drove through the streets of Lagos, which were still bustling, even at 11 p.m. on a Tuesday night. Ore and I were both struck by the experience, me as it was my first time in sub-Saharan Africa, and her as it was her first time home in years.

After driving down some not-so-friendly-looking streets, we came to our hotel. The guards there waved a wand under our car and checked the trunk before opening the gates. The hotel's lobby was very clean and cool. Check-in went smoothly for the most part, but the clerk asked for my Marriott Rewards number, which I had no idea about. I searched through my Gmail archives a bit but couldn't find it. He was willing to settle for the last 4 digits I found in one email (they had unhelpfully X'd out the rest in the email). Soon we were in our room for our well-deserved rest.

As it worked out, we fell asleep just after midnight, so our sleep schedule was almost shifted to normal for the next day.

Wednesday

It was a hot summer day in Lagos! Well, not by their standards, but by mine it sure was. The sun was so bright I even opted for sunglasses. We took our time getting ready and then walked to the mall a block away from our hotel to try to reactivate Ore's SIM card. We went into the Airtel store, which was far too small for the number of people waiting there. And more people kept coming in.

After about forty-five minutes of waiting, we found out that Ore couldn't reactivate her SIM card without a fee since she had not used it for three years. So, we walked to her bank's nearest branch to get some money out.

We were near the center of Ikeja, where a lot of government offices are located. We walked by the Lagos IRS and the City Planners' Association on the way. I got to see more of the lively streets on the way. Lots of yellow taxi vans and street vendors selling water, bread, and fruit. All of the taxis would honk as they passed me. I thought they just honked a lot, but Ore said they were trying to get my attention specifically. Ore told me that one person called out, "How ya doing, oyinbo?" But it blended in with the ambient noise to my ears (like a typical oyinbo, I guess). Only one kid walked next to us for quite a while and kept begging for money. "That's very annoying, stop that," said Ore, and he gave up.

Having been to India was good preparation for Nigeria. So far, Nigeria actually seemed less chaotic.

The bank had high security. We had to pass through a little capsule-type metal detector to get in. The bank's lobby was very cool and clean. They had a brochure advertising their military bank accounts that featured an image of Nigerian soldiers planting their flag together, Iwo Jima–style.

Soon we learned that before she could get her money out, Ore needed to get a BVN (Bank Verification Number). The number seemed pointless to me, but you need one for Nigerian banking now. This resulted in a lot of paperwork and a lot more waiting. They had a nice and cool waiting room in the branch that I could sit in, thankfully. After about an hour and fifteen minutes the power went out, and I experienced my first one of Nigeria's famous blackouts. The bank's generators kicked in pretty quickly though, so no problems.

Ore ran into a problem at the bank, though. Her bank had her middle name abbreviated in its records, but it is spelled out in full on her passport. To get the BVN number, she had to have them standardized. In addition to filling out forms, she also had to handwrite a letter asking for it. Unfortunately, in her first draft, she wrote her name first-middle-last, but the bank insisted on a second draft with it written last-first-middle for inscrutable reasons.

Then we went back to the room briefly and hopped in a taxi to go to Ore's mom's daycare. I was assured that the taxi was ripping us off. Once again, I wondered if everyone was ripping us off, was anyone really ripping us off? The taxi took us further outside the center of the city, so I got to see more of the real Lagos.

When we got to the daycare, I got to meet Ore's brother Solomon and Ore's nephew Ayo. Ore was thrilled to see Solomon again. It was a touching reunion. We hung out there for a while and chatted with Ore's mom and brother for a while. There were some little boys around at the daycare, they were very friendly and cute. We got to see the traditional clothes for the wedding, and I tried mine on. They fit well.

We needed to change money, and Ore's mom knew how to get us the best rate. It turns out that there are some Northern tribesmen in the city that hang out on the road and change money out of tiny offices. Despite not being an official bank, it is allegedly legal. They were the first tribesmen I'd met so far on the trip. At one point, they brought another guy into the offices to look at an expensive-looking gold ring. Ore thought it was probably stolen and being pawned.

They gave us a rate of 358 to the dollar. The rate Google gave was 362, but that's the bank-to-bank rate, I thought. So, it was actually a pretty good deal. The ATM in the hotel lobby gave me a rate of 305 when I took out money to pay the taxi there, for comparison.

The only problem was that we were changing $700, and they had nowhere near the conversion of 250,000 naira on them. They told Ore's mom that they would bank transfer the naira to her, and she could withdraw it from her ATM. They made the bank transfer, but she didn't see it appear in her account. They waited a while, checking again and again on her phone for the confirmation. It didn't come in, so they walked off to the ATM to check if it was available there yet. It wasn't.

We walked back to the tribesman's tiny office and sat awkwardly for a while, each side trying to figure out what to do. The man who sent the money transfer came over for the first time and talked intensely with Ore's mom for a while. They both came with us to the ATM to check it a few more times. Then they stood around arguing for a while about what to do. Ore's mom really held her own. They eventually agreed that she would keep the cash until the transfer posts, and she would show them where she lives in case she never got back to them. After showing them where she worked, they finally went on their way. (The next day I learned that the transfer posted an hour or so after we left, and she walked by to give them the dollars without an issue.)

After hanging out for a little while longer, we got in a car to go home. The driver was a friend of Ore's mom. We stopped at a Tastee restaurant and got some food. I ordered the plantains and bean-cake. The bean-cake had fish in them, so I didn't have any because I'm a vegetarian. At that point, all I had eaten that day was bread and plantains. After arriving at the hotel, I figured that I'd treat myself to some room service dessert to make up for it. When we called, they were out of all the desserts except the raw fruit. So Ore ate the fruit, and I skipped dessert.

Thursday

Thursday was our market day, and my parents and brother's arrival day. Ore's mom told us she'd come by at 8 a.m. to get an early start to our market trip, so I set a 6:30 alarm. After getting up, I decided to check out the hotel buffet before we left. It was a pretty solid spread, and it had plenty of much-needed coffee. The buffet was $14, which is almost unheard of by Nigerian standards. (Note: The next day we found out that there was one free breakfast per room each day. So it was only $14 if we both ate.)

Ore's mom got to the hotel early—no "African time" here! She had the first installment of our N250,000. Due to ATM restrictions, she could only take out N100,000 per day. From the hotel, we left for our market day.

On the way, I got to see more of the city, and some of the morning traffic. First, we drove to an ATM to work on getting the rest of the cash. Then we drove toward Ore's grandmother's house. We passed through the Yaba neighborhood on the way, where the wedding would be. Yaba has a reputation as being the tough part of town. They said this wasn't the bad part of Yaba; it looked a little rough, though. On the way there we passed a building that once contained a hospital, the one where Ore was born.

The University of Lagos was on the way, so we swung by there. There were some nice student buildings and statues there. And there were a lot of posters for student associations, as well as a surprising number warning against cults. Ore said that a lot of the cults recruit students. (Note: I later learned that Nigerian cults are more equivalent to street gangs than Scientology, or the groups we call cults in the West.) We saw a track at the campus, so we stopped and asked the attendant about the possibility of using it. He said it was open to the public for a small fee, so we resolved to go back to run when we had more time.

We arrived at Ore's grandmother's house a short drive later. It is a decent sized two-story building. Ore's relatives live in one unit and they rent out the others. From what I recall, her grandmother and grandfather were pretty well off. Ore's grandfather is buried in a tomb on the same land, so I saw that as well.

Ore's ninety-three-year-old grandmother was out and about when we got there. She is a tiny lady, but she's very energetic and active. She was very happy to see us once Ore's mother explained who we were. She is only fluent in Yoruba, unfortunately, so we didn't get to have much of a conversation.

We went into the house and met Ore's aunt and cousin, who were very nice. Ore's aunt was working on the dresses for the wedding, so Ore got to try hers on. She commended me on my perfect pronunciation of Ore's name. I was extremely proud of myself and afraid to pronounce her name again. There were some pictures of Ore's grandfather there. I found them fascinating to see. I met another of Ore's cousins as well. The power went out while we were there, so we hung out in the dark, which was a very normal situation for them. A friend of Ore's mother stopped by; she was going to be the MC for the wedding. She was to accompany us on our trip to the market.

Before we left, I snapped a picture of Ore with her mother and grandmother. It was amazing to see three generations in one picture like that.

From there we drove to the market. Our first stop was the rice market. There were fairly large buildings that Ore's mom and her friend went into, almost like warehouses. We stayed in the car for this part. It took them a long time in there, making me wonder if they were inspecting grains of rice or something.

While we were waiting, an SUV and a car pulled up with a new delivery. They had custom suspensions on them, so their rear ends were lifted incredibly high. It looked like something out of Mad Max. Then they started pulling out fifty-kilo bags of rice and putting them on their heads! I really wanted to take pictures, but it struck me as impolite to do so. They were just average guys hard at work; it wasn't a tourist destination.

It was around midday, so Ore bought some frozen yogurt from a vendor while we waited. It would be the last food I ate till 10 p.m.

From the rice wholesaler, we went to the market itself. Actually, to one market of many. It seemed like there was a large geographic area full of sprawling markets. Of this large area, Ore's mom had a few specific small shops she wanted to go to. We parked in an old bank parking lot, which was actually the bank she used to work in, I think. That branch is closed now and serves as a parking area for the markets.

We walked a short distance to the market and sought out our preferred yam seller. There was a makeshift wooden structure with plastic roofing around these vendors. There was an incredible number of yams. The first place we went to wasn't giving them a very good price, so we walked off to another one. There was a lot of talking and waiting, but Ore's mom and her friend got the price they wanted in the end. The vendor had a seat I could rest on while they talked. I had been told in no uncertain terms not to flash my camera around in the bustling market, but I was now in a secure location, so I took some pictures. After we had agreed on a price (after lots of negotiating), they loaded the yams in two baskets and boys hoisted them on their heads and walked the five minutes to the car with us.

We walked to another market area next. It was a short way from the yam market in the other direction. It had a larger main strip to walk through. It was amazing to look down it and see all the activities. It would have made an awesome picture. There was also a storefront with live goats tied up. I wanted to buy them all and set them free, but I didn't. We walked down a side path from the market to a series of quiet wood stalls. There we met a lady who sells all kinds of nuts and peppers. They bought a number of things from her. They seemed to know her better than the other sellers, so there was a lot of sitting around and chatting and no hard bargaining.

After that, we left the market and made our way back to Ore's grandmother's house. We unloaded all the food at the house. I tried to help as much as I could. It was actually kind of fun to deadlift and carry a big bag of rice. We said goodbye to Ore's relatives and drove off.

I wanted to head right to the airport since my mom and dad were arriving at 4, but Ore's mom and her friend (our MC) said they would stop at one place first. Before that, we stopped to pick up the MC's son. He was pretty quiet and didn't say anything to us. Then we drove to a basket market to buy some for the ceremony. At this point, I was really starting to think we needed to leave for the airport, but I didn't want to be rude or anything. I casually mentioned the time the flight was arriving a few times, but they were unconcerned, saying we had plenty of time. We looked at the baskets for a bit longer, and then I pointed out the time again. This time, Ore's mom agreed that it was time to go but said we were close to the airport so no need to worry.

There was need to worry; we drove straight into a traffic jam and moved at a walking pace for forty-five minutes. When we got to the airport, I realized that there was no curbside pickup so we would have to park in the economy lot and take a shuttle to the terminal.

By the time we got to mom and dad, they had been waiting outside the terminal for forty-five minutes. They were very happy to see us. I was mortified. A nice man had been keeping them company while they waited, for a fee I soon realized.

We brought them back to the hotel and they got safely checked in. Then Ore went and bought a SIM card before we went back to the airport to meet Eric's flight. Eric's situation was the reverse from mom and dad's, we waited outside the terminal for a long time before he came out. We caught him right as he came out, though.

Soon, we were all checked in and resting at the hotel.

Saturday

The night before the wedding, our on-call tailor had told us that he would finish the alterations around midnight and then hightail it to our hotel. We tried to stay up late to meet him, but I was asleep by midnight. At 1 a.m., Ore talked to him on the phone, and he said he'd be done with the clothes at about 4 a.m. Ore decided that she would take a quick nap till then.

I woke up at 5:50, hearing Ore talking to the tailor. He was close at that point. We walked out to meet the tailor at the gate. The front gate attendant said, "Good morning, Master" to me. I found that oddly unsettling. The tailor arrived shortly, and we relayed the clothes to my dad and brother. Thankfully, these clothes fit fine.

My dad and brother were still missing cufflinks though, so the tailor volunteered to pick some up for them. We gave him money for the cufflinks and bus fare and sent him on his way.

We grabbed a quick breakfast just before seven. Lola, a classmate of Ore's who does makeup on the side, showed up promptly at seven. We had decided that she would do my mom's makeup first, so we took the elevator up to my parents' floor. They weren't there. Baffled, I walked down to the breakfast buffet again, and there they were. They had gone down the stairs as we were coming up the elevator. We set her up with Lola and went down for our breakfast.

The photographer showed up early. Unfortunately, no one was ready yet, so he had to wait for a bit. After the guys got ready, he took a few individual pictures of us in the hallway. Ore's makeup and gele (a traditional head-tie) took longer than we thought, so they had to wait for her. We rushed in a few good pictures together before we had to leave.

Since we were supposed to be "getting married," we had to arrive at the site in separate cars. We booked Ubers since we had found them to be cheaper and more reliable than the taxis there. We had meant to leave early in case of traffic but left with just enough time to get there if there was no traffic. Thankfully, there was none, and we got there on time.

When we arrived at the site, a bodybuilder in a security uniform opened the gate for our car. Ore's car was already there even though she had left after us. I got out of our car and walked into Ore's Uber, where she was waiting. "My dad is here!" she exclaimed, "And he brought his whole family! Did you tell him? Did you tell him we were having it here?" I profusely denied doing so, which satisfied her. I entered panic mode immediately.

She sent me out to tell my parents what was going on, and not to talk to or touch anyone. I walked over to them, but Ore's dad had already gotten to them and asked why they weren't returning his calls. I think they blamed technical difficulties on Facebook Messenger.

I went back into Ore's car. They were having a lot of trouble paying the Uber driver since the network was going down (a common problem, which stops Uber Nigeria from being as hassle-free as it is elsewhere). Ore noted that her dad had brought his own food, drinks, and caterers.

We had all arrived at the venue on time for the planned 11 a.m., no African time, start of the ceremony. But it would not start for a while yet.

We were soon shown to a small side room with five seats, a small bathroom, and, most importantly, an air conditioner. Ore had given strict instructions that only people with invitations be allowed to enter the function hall. Thus far, our team of impressively sized security men was holding back those without them.

A few people came in to briefly visit with us in the side room we had. Ore's brother Solomon was there with his camera, and my family got to meet him for the first time.

Then Ore's dad came in. He started yelling about all his grievances, repeating much of what he had told me over the phone a few months ago in a more concise way. We stood and listened for a while. He only paused to take one phone call during his angry lecture.

He had some specific comments about the venue setting, which were lost on me. I do know that he wanted the bouncers to go away and let his family take the best seats.

At one point, Ore started to interrupt him to argue about one point, so I raised my hands (and voice) to jump in between them. "You've said your piece," I interjected, "now let us discuss our response." He said he would, and my dad spoke up about how as Christians we should seek the ministry of reconciliation. Ore's dad liked this idea and shook hands with my dad. He then told Ore he forgave her for what she did and gave her a hug. Or tried to—she pulled away a fair bit when he hugged her.

We were all pretty mad and shaken up when he left. Ore's mom came in a short time later and talked it over with Ore. They discussed how to handle the seating and access to her dad's family. Ore's mother's cousin came in and argued with them loudly over how to handle it, preferring to do something closer to her dad's way. Ore was very worried that her dad's family would try to put some kind of witchcraft or voodoo on us.

After she left, we sat and then prayed together for a bit. A nice friend of Ore's mom was with us in the room. She kept us company as well. I am uncertain about all the details about how the seating conflict was worked out, but Ore's dad and some senior relatives were in seats of honor across from Ore's mom's relatives. Other members of his group were in the back.

A number of Ore's friends and relatives filed into the room to visit with us. We had plenty of time to meet with them since the wedding was starting so late. Ore's sister Tumi came in at one point. It was nice to finally meet her. She had run really late getting ready and had to leave early for an exam. (I'd never heard of an exam on a Saturday afternoon before.) So, she was only able to greet us quickly and then go. Her son peeked in too. He was in very cute native attire.

Ore's MC came in to say hi, along with an MC for our family. Traditionally, each family will hire an MC, so they hired one for us. She joked that it made sense for her to be our MC because she had a pointy nose like ours. I heard that Ore's dad brought an MC, but I don't think they let her perform.

At about 1 p.m., two hours after the supposed start time, my family was ushered up to the hall for the start of the ceremony. Ore and I were each to remain in the room for a while before making separate entrances. I'm not completely sure of everything that went on before I came up. My parents later told me that they found it a little overwhelming, with the heat and the noise. It was very crowded in the hall since we had only planned on half the attendees that came.

My family was supposed to dance into the event. After they entered the MC asked my dad, "Who are you dancing for?" My dad confidently replied, "Jesus!" He was supposed to say the name of the groom. Oops. They were asked to give money at a number of junctures in the ceremony. This is somewhat traditional, but the staff may have added some extra requests. And they started asking them to give in dollars as well. This all led up to the portion of the event where my relatives bowed to Ore's family.

The MCs talked loudly and rapidly. Often it seemed that they were arguing with each other. Then they would break into song. Many of the songs were Christian worship songs that I recognized. At one point, our MC suddenly gave a heartfelt, if somewhat mangled, rendition of "Take Me Home, Country Roads." Sadly, I was not there to witness that.

I was brought up to the hall at about 1:30. Two of Ore's cousins walked in with me, to play the role of my friends in the ceremony. They also gave me directions at confusing points in the service.

We walked up the stairs and into the ceremony. I doffed my cap as I went in. This was to emphasize that I was walking in humbly, as I was asking them for the hand of their daughter. When I entered the hall, they asked me my name and who it was that I wished to marry. Then I danced for a bit. I tried to dance really low as I had seen before. I gave people money a few times. They had given me a stack of 500s to give one by one. These were exhausted pretty quickly.

Next, they had me stand in front of Ore's parents. This led to the prostration portion of the ceremony, in which I bowed to the floor three times. On the third time, I was told to grab the ankles of the parents. I stayed down on the floor for a while and they prayed for me.

When I got up, they had me empty my pockets to symbolize a down payment on land in Nigeria. Next, they had me sit on the couch between different relatives while they took pictures.

After this, I was mercifully allowed to go to my seat. They had a couch on a platform with decorations around it for Ore and me to sit on.

Now it was finally time for Ore to come in. There was a lot of singing to welcome her in. Ore came in wearing a veil. They sang and danced around her. She did kneel to her parents at one point. She was asked to explain her intentions in Yoruba, which she struggled with—to their amusement. "She went to America and she forgot her language!" they exclaimed.

At the conclusion of her introduction, they told her that one year from now she should have a baby. They let us sit together on the couch after that. When she arrived on the couch, she put my cap back on my head.

They then brought out the engagement letter that we had prepared for Ore's family. A cousin of Ore's read it. She only struggled a little with the elegant cursive calligraphy. Ore's parents gave their consent to the union, and we had no more worries. They in return gave us a letter of acceptance (which I didn't realize till later).

While we were on the couch, they asked Ore to choose her favorite present of all the gifts. As per tradition, she picked the Bible (which was actually hers from home). There was a bow tied to it, with her engagement and wedding rings tied to it. I undid the bow and put the ring on her finger.

Ore's mother's pastor came up and prayed. Then they had me pick Ore up and dance while holding her.

Next, people came up to take pictures with us. We hugged and greeted a lot of people. Eventually, they let us go downstairs to return to the air-conditioned room. But before that, we went table to table and greeted Ore's relatives. She had trouble placing a number of them, especially the ones her dad had brought. While we did this, our enormous security guard walked a step behind us, as he would for the rest of the evening.

Then we reentered the small, cool room we had waited in before the ceremony. We just sat and relaxed for a little while. Then Ore's mom brought us some salad and a few types of rice. My appetite was pretty much gone, what with all the heat and stress. Ore was quite insistent that I eat something, so I had a little jollof rice.

We sat and rested for a while and took a few pictures of ourselves with our phones. They brought us some nice cool water as well. A few more people stopped in to say hi too. I went out of the room to say thanks to our security men and get a quick picture with them. Soon enough, we decided to go out to take more group pictures with our photographer.

They brought us up to the event hall to take pictures on the stage. On the way, my dad and I took pictures with Ore's dad. That made her dad very happy. Ore didn't pause at all and walked right up the stairs.

While we were downstairs, Ore's mom's family was splitting up the ceremonial gifts we gave them to take home. They had tried to split a jug of palm oil but had spilled it all over the floor. We went up to the stage, taking care to avoid stepping in the oil. We took turns standing on the stage in groups for pictures. After we got a few, my mom started feeling pretty bad. She said she was trying hard not to get sick. It turned out that she was just feeling overwhelmed by the heat. At that point, we decided to call it a night.

We walked down to the street-level pavilion to wait while Ore's cousin called a cab. He called a friend of his so he could vouch for his honesty. This took a little longer than he had hoped, but he got there in about fifteen minutes. We put my family into the cab and sent them off.

Next up, Ore and I had to get transport. We told our personal giant who seemingly waded into the crowds of people and cars on the street and pulled a taxi back for us.

Overall, the terms of the wedding worked out ok for us. In fact, it was kind of like the hard-negotiating sessions that dominate much of Nigerian life.

One thing my husband said to me after our trip to Nigeria that stayed with me was that visiting Nigeria and seeing me in my homeland made him understand me a little better. Us Nigerians tend to be quite tough, and that is usually seen in the way we bargain at the markets. We had been married for just eight months when we made the trip and were still trying to figure out how marriage worked. The Nigerian wedding ended up quite stressful for us, but we were used to these challenges. Being from two different countries with two completely different backgrounds, it was quite an interesting first year. Our trip to Nigeria was such a bonding experience for us as a couple. And for me, it was such a rewarding experience being able to share a piece of my culture with my husband and my in-laws.

My dear husband was very adventurous about riding on motorcycle driven by a crazy driver and touring the markets and the city, but not very adventurous with the food despite my assurance that he was very unlikely to get food poisoning. He chose to err on the side of caution, which was his loss. But I did the exact opposite because I hadn't had authentic Nigerian street food in three years. I was not going to let the opportunity to indulge pass me by.

I appreciate the beauty that is culture. There's a kind of bond and understanding you develop with people when you experience a part of their culture. There is certainly something to be said about being open to hearing and learning about cultures and traditions outside of our own. It can help us rid our minds of false stereotypes. And showing genuine interest in and sharing a piece of someone's culture has a way of opening our hearts toward them in understanding as well as a building a sense of brotherhood.

IMMIGRANT MENTALITY

I DON'T BELIEVE ANYONE LEAVES their home country for another country without a good reason. It's not a decision anyone takes lightly.

Immigrants often have to leave behind family, lifelong friends, stability, livelihood, houses, and other properties. Some have to leave their children and spouse behind in order to make money to give their family a better life; it can often be more challenging to bring the family along.

It's easy to judge people and clamor for the government to refuse to let immigrants in without knowing people's stories and the hardship some of them face in their countries. Families are being torn apart by civil wars, tribal wars, and economic crises. Many people leave their countries not because they want to but because they need to. Some leave in search of hope. Others leave selflessly because they can't imagine their children living through what they lived through or are living through. So, people leave their homes, their extended family if they have any left, and all that is familiar to venture into a foreign environment.

Many times, as immigrants, we end up having to pick up odd jobs to sustain ourselves. After all, the bills won't wait for us to find the job of our dreams. So, many immigrants do these odd jobs on a daily basis to survive. But for those who were working in professional settings prior to their move to another country, these jobs can seem very odd indeed.

I remember having to pick up a couple of these odd jobs while I waited to find a pharmacist position. I had applied to several jobs, and as the hopeful immigrant that I am, I figured it would take a month or two to receive that call offering me a job. That was not the case.

Two months became three. Three months became four when I decided to apply for jobs outside of pharmacy. I applied to a few, and it did not take long to get an employment offer as a bus monitor. I had no idea what that meant, but it sounded interesting. So, I accepted the offer. All I had to do was sit on the school bus and keep an eye on the children that got on the bus, as well as ensure they don't fall while getting off the bus. It was a job that turned out to be quite depressing for me in one way and uplifting in another.

The particular school bus system I worked in catered to kids with special needs and varying levels of disability. I saw some children, two in particular, with extreme mental and physical disabilities such that they had to be strapped into the bus seat because they could not sit on their own without support. Some were in wheelchairs which had to be anchored to the floor of the bus. I tried not to stare. In Nigeria, we usually avoid eye contact with people with disabilities because we were taught as children that it was rude to look at them or point at them. There is a fine line between looking and staring, so I was careful not to stare during bus monitoring even though I wanted to look at them and take in their various features and learn more about them.

Working as a bus monitor was amazing to see to say the least. I wondered how these kids could survive all these years. I was told they were in their early teenage years so that meant at least a decade of extra care and nurturing from parents or guardians. Even with the drooling and jerky movements, the kids looked like they were happy and well cared for. Thinking about the mental and financial investments from the parents or guardians of these kids was shocking. Nigeria has the complete opposite attitude regarding those with disabilities, which is a sad truth.

It was remarkable to think about the dedication of these kids' parents. I began to imagine the sheer expense of caring for a disabled child let alone two, like from the one family. There were the special wheelchairs, hiring a physical therapist and other home care, hospital bills, and so on. Yet, some people are gracious enough to do it happily.

Though, there was one child whose mother was always smoking when we came to drop her off at home. She would come out of the house with a lit cigarette hanging from one corner of her mouth. It was disgusting to see and quite depressing to know that such a young child was being exposed to secondhand smoke and the carcinogens that come with it. *How can a mother be so selfish? How can any parent, really?*

All of these experiences made me wonder if I had it in me to care for a disabled child. As a bus monitor, I saw a few children with Down syndrome up close for the first time in my life. Each time the bus would stop to pick them up in the mornings, I would briefly study the face of their parent and wonder how they and their families managed so graciously. It must be tough, but the families' dedication and deep love for their children was evident with all the love, energy, and resources they put forth. That was uplifting.

To make it in time to pick the kids from their respective homes and take them to school on time, the bus driver would pick me up at home by 5:45 a.m., and we would drive around town picking kids from their homes and to school till about 10 a.m. when he would drop me off at home. He would return to pick me up at 3 p.m. and we would drive around town again to pick up another set of children from their various schools and take them back home.

I spent about ten hours a week or so being a bus monitor, and I felt I needed to take on a second job to be able to bring more money in. I still had the bank loan I'd taken for graduate school to pay off. It was hard to get another job that would fit around the odd schedule of the bus monitor job. Ideally, I would need a job I could start around 11 a.m., work till shortly before 3 p.m., then be back on the job at 5 p.m. or so when I got off the bus. That didn't seem feasible. I kept looking anyway.

A few weeks after, I was able to find a job as a newspaper delivery person. This position required me to be up at 2:20 a.m. to get to the newspaper warehouse at 3 a.m. At the warehouse, there were actually other humans out and about and ready to deliver papers at 3 a.m. I learned that a few of them were retirees looking to keep themselves busy, some were full-time housewives looking to bring in some money in the wee hours of the night while the kids were still asleep, and others were people like me who just needed a supplemental income.

It was early winter when I started the newspaper delivery gig. A few days into the job, I realized that my terrible sense of direction was actually worse than I'd thought it was. I never thought a lot more went into newspaper delivery. I've only seen newspapers delivered on TV, where a young lad on his bicycle throws newspapers onto people's porches with perfect aim.

But it wasn't that easy in real life. First of all, it was winter, and there was no riding a bike to deliver papers in such weather. Secondly, elderly people tend to be very picky about where they want their newspapers delivered. I was given a long list of addresses to deliver to with specific instructions on where the newspapers had to be placed. Some people were fine with just tossing it in the driveway (my favorite). Others wanted it on the side porch, some on the front porch, some in between the storm door and main door, some on the third step from the bottom. The preferences were endless.

My first day on the job, I went with one of the managers, and it took about two hours. He had been doing it for years, so he could probably do it with his eyes closed. He told me I would soon be able to identify the houses by their different features, such as a truck parked out front or the color. I wasn't sure how I would be able to make out the color of a house in the dark, but I was optimistic. I was back home by 5 a.m., then showered and got ready for the bus. I was quite exhausted and tried very hard to stay awake on the bus.

The next day I had to do the delivery alone. It took me four hours. In fact, at the four-hour mark, I still wasn't finished and still had a few houses to deliver to. I got a call from the manager asking if I needed help. I said yes, and he asked where I was and came to meet me. With his help, I got through the rest of the deliveries in no time. The next day I was told the office got a few complaints. One was a complaint about the newspaper not being placed in the spot they requested. Another was that they did not receive their newspaper. I guess that's why I had three extra newspapers at the end of my delivery. Oops.

I was more careful the next day and tried not to miss any delivery. It took me another four-plus hour on my own. I was feeling quite proud of myself that I delivered all the papers except the one I got to keep as a perk of being a newspaper lady. There was another complaint waiting for me the next day, though. This time the complaint was that I'd taken too long to deliver the newspaper to a house. The manager said most people preferred their newspapers to be delivered while it was still dark, and ideally before 6 a.m. The next day I set out again. Luckily, schools happened to be on a short winter break for Thanksgiving, so for a few days, I was able to rest after waking up at 2:30 a.m. to deliver papers, rather than get on the bus to take kids to school.

Delivering newspapers on Thanksgiving Day was an absolute nightmare. It so happens that everyone got a newspaper, including those who do not typically get newspapers daily since they did not sign up. A courtesy sort of delivery as I understood it. The newspapers also had to have ads and coupons to go with them, so I spent my first hour in the warehouse stuffing coupons and ads into about a hundred newspapers. Luckily, one of the managers volunteered to meet up with me later to give me a hand with the delivery. He could tell I was struggling with the job. I was so exhausted after the Thanksgiving Day delivery that I wondered what insanity prompted me to take on this job in the first place.

Given my sense of direction, delivering papers in daylight would be a hassle, but doing it in the middle of the cold, winter nights was more than I could handle. It was so stressful jumping out of my car to throw papers onto people's porches or slide them into tight spaces and then having to jog back to my car, drive a minute or two and repeat the same thing in the next address. It did not help that some of the houses did not have their numbers clear enough for me to make out the numbers in the middle of the night, with only the streetlights as the source of illumination. If the houses I had to deliver to were side by side, I would grab several papers and jog all the way to deliver them and end up having to jog back a longer distance back to my car. I decided to scout that neighborhood during broad daylight and then record myself describing the different features of the houses I had to deliver to or the ones closest to them.

It was strange to be driving around the neighborhood during the day, and they obviously looked nothing like they did at 3:30 a.m. It was almost Christmas, so several houses had Christmas decorations and lights outside. I used some of the decorations as descriptions in my audio. My description and direction to myself went something like this: "Drive one minute and stop at house with Mary and baby Jesus decoration outside, skip house and deliver paper to next house…give paper to house on the left, put on front porch…drive to house with number fifty-seven, put paper in mail slot…drive past house with red flashing Christmas light decoration and count two houses after that, deliver paper on side porch…" I had solicited my husband's help with this mission, and he did the driving, while I, with the help of my delivery list, was able to determine which houses received newspapers. I recorded an audio of step-by-step directions that I hoped would help guide me on my next delivery. My next delivery took about three and a half hours.

Although I felt that it took too much time to pause and resume the audio, the audio recording helped somewhat. It didn't significantly reduce my delivery time but at least I did not feel like I was reaching around in the dark trying to locate the houses as I had in the previous days. Later that week, I texted the manager to let him know I was quitting. It had only been three weeks, but I just couldn't do it anymore. School was back on and I could not risk taking so long delivering papers that I ended up missing the bus when the driver came to get me.

I went back to applying for jobs again and got a full-time job as a paraeducator for students with mental disabilities. Their ages ranged from about five or to about eighteen. With the full-time job, I wouldn't be able to continue as a bus monitor, so I resigned.

The school was about an hour away from home, and there was a mandatory week of orientation before starting the job. At the orientation, we were taught some self-defense maneuvers to use if we were attacked by one of the students. We were told that since they had mental disabilities, they had a tendency to display irrational behaviors, such as suddenly sprinting away for no reason, biting, hair pulling, and so on. That made me ask a lot of questions. I remember the particularly surprising response to one question.

"What if you know they are about to bolt? Can you hold them to stop them from running into danger, such as oncoming traffic or from running into the woods?"

Nope.

Okay.

By the end of my first week of orientation, I knew my heart could not take working in a setting like that. On one of the last days of orientation, we were told to spend a few hours in the classrooms we would be assigned to, and I spent a couple of hours watching a young boy try to slam his head on his desk. It clearly wasn't his first time because there was special padding that had been placed there to prevent him from hurting himself. There was another who tried to run out of the class, yet another who kept throwing himself on the floor, and then one who kept screaming at the top of his lungs for no apparent reason. One of the people I was attending orientation with told me she would not be coming back the next day to complete the orientation.

Two days before the end of orientation, I received an email from a recruiter inviting me for an interview for a pharmacist position in a retail chain. I accepted, of course. That was the sign I needed to tender my resignation. I had just done one week of orientation and no actual work yet, but I thought the right thing to do was to officially resign with a letter to the HR department.

Working with that group of children involved a ton of rules and a lot of caution. Many of these children had been through a lot of abuse. For some of them, that was what led to their current mental state, and for others, the abuse was because of their disability. Sometimes, I just wonder why the world is such a crappy place, and it vexes my spirit to think about what so many innocent children go through.

I've heard it said that Black people in America have to work twice as hard to prove that they can do just as well as a white person with equal or less qualification. Well, in that case, immigrants have to work four times as hard to prove that we can do the job as well, if not better than anyone else with the same qualifications. One of the challenges we face is our "Before America" experience not counting towards our job experience. Employers in America want to see US-based work experience. That in itself already puts us at a disadvantage. When we take equivalency exams, it shows that our foreign education actually does match up with American education, yet many times employers prefer to see a US-based education, which is yet another disadvantage.

During my six-month job search after I became a licensed pharmacist in the US, I was told several things when it came to my resume. I had been applying to several jobs without any luck, so I reached out to other Nigerians on LinkedIn whose profile showed that they had also studied pharmacy in Nigeria before moving to the US. I reasoned that they were in a better position to give me advice than a Nigerian who studied pharmacy in the US. I got a lot of responses and advice. I sent them my resume hoping that they could perhaps fish out the flaws in it that were preventing me from getting a job.

One man stressed the fact that I had to remove all my Nigeria-related work experience from my resume. He said it was useless in the US and that no employer cared to see it. I made a duplicate resume in which I removed all my Nigerian work experience. Suffice to say that my resume looked as scanty as an empty refrigerator. Even I would not want to hire me with that kind of resume. I spoke with another lady who when I told her what the other man had advised, said, "That's nonsense! You should include your Nigerian work experience, otherwise, your resume will appear empty." She added that she had included her Nigerian work experience prior to getting her first job in the US, and she had eventually been hired, so she did not believe including my Nigerian experience was hurting my resume in any way. I decided to leave my foreign work experience on my resume and eventually, after the long discouraging wait, I had a job.

For me, it is not enough to have a job. I want to be happy going to work rather than dreading a stressful day fielding calls from angry patients wondering why they cannot get their opioids filled too early, or people coming to ask me what size of condoms I would recommend for them. Sorry, Billy, I don't know or care about your penis size.

When I express my dislike for my job, some people are quick to say, "At least you have a job." Yes, I have a job and I'm thankful for it. I don't believe that being thankful means I should settle for less than what I want, though. Sure, some people don't have jobs—that doesn't mean I should not aspire for a better and more fulfilling job. If other people want to settle into their comfort zones, that's their business, not mine. I did not leave my well-paying job and my family behind in Nigeria, or empty out my life's savings to move to a foreign country only to settle for whatever I can get. If I wanted to settle for what was comfortable, I would have stayed back in my country. I have a master's degree, and soon, I'll add a doctorate degree. And I'm far from done. I still have my eye on different certifications and degrees.

To some, it may appear that I don't really know what I want. But I do. I want to be able to pick and choose what job offers I accept. I want to develop as many skills as possible so that I become valuable to any employer without holding on to an unfulfilling job just because it pays very well and provides financial security. My investment in higher education is a way to position myself for better opportunities that would gradually move me closer to my dream job. I am not unique in this quest for continuous education and lifelong learning. Data has shown that Nigerians have the highest levels of education in the US and are the most educated immigrant group in the US.[1,2]

I have heard this—Nigerian immigrants' quest to continue attaining educational advancement—labelled as *the immigrant mentality*. Immigrant mentality as I've heard it described, is the relentless, self-motivated ambition of immigrants. According to the US Census Bureau, 61.4% of Nigerians aged twenty-five and older had a bachelor's degree or higher compared with 28.5% of the total US population.[1,2] Four percent of Nigerians hold a PhD compared to 1% of the general US population, and 29% of Nigerians have graduate degrees compared to 11% of the overall American population. Seventeen percent of Nigerians hold a master's degree, while only 8% of the white population in the US does. And 37% of Nigerians have a bachelor's degree compared to 19% of the general US population.

Oftentimes, it gets discouraging that with all the learning we do and degrees we acquire, we still have to prove that we're smart enough to be hired. We apply for jobs that we are more than qualified for, but we don't even get invited for an interview.

A few years ago, while still pursuing my master's degree, I heard someone say, "When the hiring manager sees that your name is a foreign name, they don't bother with your resume. We need to change our names to Sally or John." This was an international student like me, so he was probably a little disgruntled about the system at the time. A part of me has always wondered if those words had an element of truth in them. It certainly feels like that sometimes. I applied to about one hundred jobs before I finally got an offer and that's not an exaggeration—I kept a spreadsheet of places I applied to. I pursued licensure in another state just to improve my chances of getting a job. Although many job postings include that a Bachelor of Pharmacy is acceptable, it did not feel like it.

I don't think that Americans or those with US-based work experience have it easy finding jobs either, but I believe they have it a little easier than immigrants do. Other factors to take into consideration is that many US undergraduate students are exposed to a lot of different opportunities, like internships, that foreign graduates are not. International students have limited options for work while studying in the US.

Although I may have to work four times as hard to prove that my foreign work experience and my higher education make me just as qualified for a position I apply for, it's hard work that I'm hopeful will pay off in the end.

To me, the immigrant mentality is really just a different mentality that differs from the average American's. Many immigrants have suffered injustice, hardship, and struggles in different ways than some Americans, so immigrants seize the opportunity to be in America with both hands and try to make the best of it. This is not to imply that Americans do not go through hardships and struggles, but the hardship and struggles someone in a war-plagued nation faces are different. The hardship and struggles faced by those with no access to clean water, good roads, electricity, food, healthcare are different.

So, oftentimes if an educated immigrant believes getting so many advanced degrees is the way to overcome financial and economic hurdles in America, then you can bet that they will do just that. When I hear things like the immigrants are coming here to steal our jobs, I roll my eyes at the sheer ridiculousness of it. Americans weren't doing those jobs before the immigrants came, so no, they did not steal jobs. The Americans did not want to do those jobs, but the immigrants were willing to. Ironically, many of those who make such statements are unemployed and living on disability and even if they were not, they are not willing to take on many of the jobs immigrants take, possibly because they think they are beneath them. Yet they complain when immigrants have jobs they don't want.

Many immigrants know that beggars can't be choosers, and they do what they can to get by or move on to the next phase of their lives. Many times, the odd jobs we take on are just steppingstones to better ones and to a more financially secure and economically stable future.

RURAL RACISM

I WILL NEVER UNDERSTAND RACISM. Why as a human being would I dislike someone else just because they are different from me? There are many reasons to dislike a person. It's understandable to dislike a person because they are mean, rude, abusive, or pompous. But disliking someone just because they belong to a particular race, sex, or social class shows a lack of intelligence. I've seen people treat their pets better than their fellow humans and that's just disgusting.

If people from other races bled purple or blue, I would understand why someone from another race would think them strange and be skeptical or be afraid of them. But we all bleed the same, and we're pretty much the same with our internal and external organs in similar places. The differences between us don't go beyond different facial bone structures and skin color. I, for one, believe that those are differences that we should bond over rather than hate each other over.

Some people have never been hurt or had any negative experience with someone from another race, but they still hate them just because of some perceived stereotype or because they've been taught to do so.

I heard one of the most disheartening things recently. A white co-worker who has a mixed-race niece asked me what I thought about an incident that happened at her niece's school. She'd taken her five-year-old niece to an extracurricular activity in school when a white girl of about the same age as her niece came up to her niece and said, "You look like a half-burned toast my mommy throws out in the trash."

My jaw fell open. "What?! A five-year-old uttered those words?"

My co-worker nodded sadly. She had looked at the coaches who were nearby when the little white girl said that, and no one said anything. She said one of them had merely shrugged, not knowing what to do. She asked me what I thought she should do.

I honestly did not have an answer. I was too shocked that a child would know how to even say such things. I wondered what worse things she had to say and what worse things she'd been taught. If at five she's spewing such hateful words, what kinds of things would she be saying at twenty-five? I blame her parents or guardians. They must be toxic people to teach a child how to say things like that. No kid learns that all by herself. She either heard it repeated so many times or was taught how to say that to a particular type of person. My advice to my co-worker was to mention it to her niece's mother and have her handle it as she sees fit. As a mother of a mixed-race child myself, if any child says racist, hateful things to my child, I will handle both the child and his or her parents or guardians.

Racism should never be ignored or treated lightly. It's a poison that spreads insidiously until people get hurt or killed. In some cases, though, racism is subtle. I was helping out another pharmacist one day when a white couple, who appeared to be in their sixties walked up to the pharmacy to request a vaccine. I went to give them forms to fill out, and the woman asked me to check on the status of one of her husband's prescriptions. As I handed her the forms, she asked who will be giving the vaccines. I told her there were two pharmacists on duty at the time, and it would be any one of us. I ignored her sour look and asked them to sit in the waiting area while they filled out the paperwork. After looking up the prescription she'd asked for, I went to give her feedback, and she said, gesturing to her husband without looking at me, "You can say it to him, he's right here."

I responded, "Well, YOU were the one who asked me the question, so I'm giving YOU the answer. He did not ask me a question." I turned to the man and asked if he wanted the prescription.

Later on, while I was back at the computer, I glanced up for no reason and found her scowling at me. If only I had been in the mood for a staring contest. I was tempted to ask her if there was a reason she was scowling at me, but I thought it might have just been one of those subjective things. She could say she was not scowling at me, and I was the one misinterpreting her stare as a scowl. Besides, she had a right to use her eyes to look at whatever she wanted to. Like we say in my country, you can't see someone giving you a bad look if you aren't looking at them too. I shook my head and decided to ignore her.

I'm more amused than bothered by the fact that in the two years I've been working for my current employer, I have only worked with another Black person once. New Hampshire happens to be one of the least diverse states in the country. Many times, I've been the only Black person around, as far as I could tell.

One morning, I answered the phone at work, and the person on the other line asked if she could speak to someone else, claiming she could not understand my accent. "There is nothing to misunderstand, I'm speaking English," was my reply.

"Can I speak to who's in charge?" she asked.

"You are speaking to her," I answered.

She paused and tried to deflect. "I'm sorry, I just have a hard time with accents."

Mental sigh. "How may I help you?" I asked yet again. She understood me just fine when she realized I would not be transferring her to anyone else. I guess my accent did not bother her after she realized she was stuck with me.

Another time, toward the end of a usual twelve-hour shift, a white man came to the pharmacy drop-off window to ask for a drug recommendation. As we spoke, he commented on my accent and asked me where I was from. I told him I was from Nigeria. He said he spent a few years in Nigeria about a decade before. He was working for an oil company at the time. I thought that was interesting. *What are the chances of meeting a white man in rural New Hampshire who'd not only visited Nigeria but lived there for a few years?* He listed some of the Nigerian tribes he knew and asked me which one I was from. He mentioned some of the slang he'd learned while he was there, and I laughed. It was so refreshing to be able to connect with a stranger over Nigerian slang.

I've met quite a few white men who have either been to Nigeria or to other parts of Africa, and we always have nice conversations about Nigeria, Africa, and how far I am from my homeland. They ask how I manage to cope with the weather, knowing that it does not get nearly as cold in my homeland as it does in northern New Hampshire.

One day I was giving a middle-aged white woman a vaccine when she asked me where I was from. We chatted briefly and at the end she said, "I don't know you, but I wish you all the very best."

Why can't we all be like that? Why can't we meet strangers who are different from us and genuinely wish them well?

It doesn't take long to dismantle stereotypes and preconceived notions. Once we get to know people a little better, oftentimes we discover they are not as bad as we make them out to be in our heads. I've observed that most of the time it is those people who have never left the comfort of their homelands that are the quickest to judge people and to believe stereotypes; they are usually the ones who turn their noses up at having people they see as "different" around an environment they consider to be "theirs."

Oddly enough, those homebodies are rarely the brightest people around and their small-mindedness shows very easily. If you have an open mind, it is impossible to visit other countries and experience their culture without appreciating their uniqueness and seeing the beauty that their seeming "difference" adds to the world. How boring and depressing the world will be without the variety of skin tones that exist and the vast number of cultures and traditions there are.

I've learned a lot living in the US for the past six years. I enjoy learning about different cultures and making friends with people that aren't like me. I certainly hope that every person I meet feels like I treat them as humans deserving of the same space I occupy and deserving of the same air I breathe. I would not want to treat anybody less than that. In a country like America, one does not even need to leave to experience a foreign culture or to develop an open mind and acceptance of others. It's all right here. Immigrants from all over the world are all around us.

I certainly hope that that five-year-old girl grows up to appreciate the beauty of every skin color and rejects all the evil and meanness that she's being fed right now. I hope that she learns to replace hatred with love. And I hope she grows to have genuine friendships with people of other races and colors. Her life will be richer for it.

BLACK VS. BLACK

I AM NO STRANGER TO prejudice. I've experienced prejudice at the hands of my own grandmother.

My first memory of spending the holidays with my grandparents was when I was six and my brother was four. Grandparents are supposed to pamper and spoil their grandchildren, but not so much with my grandmother. Her husband, my grandfather, was a gentle, soft-spoken man. The only thing I remember about him is that he loved to watch wrestling and circus performances on TV. I remember that every evening during the few weeks we spent at their house, after coming home from work, he would sit on his favorite brown leather chair and turn the TV on. He would watch the evening news and then tune in to watch wrestling. After that was over, he would watch circus shows for the rest of the night. My brother and I would sit quietly on another leather sofa across from him and watch wrestling too. Sometimes I would sneak looks at my grandfather, trying to figure out who he was. I rarely heard him speak. He was a very quiet man. I remember him being nice even though I don't remember ever having a conversation with him.

My grandmother, on the other hand, was not very kind. Or should I say *is* since she still lives. She would cook stew that was too spicy for our young taste buds to handle then insist we did not drink water until we were done eating. She would serve the food hot and stand over us demanding we start eating right away. I did not like hot meals and still don't. It's no fun getting one's tongue scalded while eating.

After our parents had dropped us off, my grandmother had taken my plastic dolls away from me. She said they were devilish and demonic, and she did not want them in her house. I'm not sure if she hid them or threw them away, but I never saw them again. I was not attached to them, so it was not a big deal to me. But my brother also had a toy that she had confiscated.

I have another picture of my grandmother forever ingrained into my memory. I'm sitting at her dining table scratching my head and my tiny body because the heat from the steamy food made me hot and uncomfortable. The food was hot and spicy, but we were not allowed to drink water until we cleared our plates. She would serve us our meal on glass plates and give us spoons made of stainless steel and demand that we must not make any noise while scooping up our food. Each time the spoon hit our teeth while eating, she would always yell, "Are your teeth and spoon fighting a war?" It would have been very easy if she had just served our meals on plastic plates or given us plastic spoons as is common with young children. But no, she would demand these unfair table manners from a six- and a four-year-old. After lunch she would serve us lime tea, which I hated. It was steaming hot and unpleasant tasting. I don't know how she made it, but I figured she must have squeezed out several lime fruits and boiled them or something because I remember the feel of the pulp in my mouth. Sometimes, she would serve us the lime tea *after* a hot, spicy meal, in place of water. I was always the last to finish my meal since I was a slow eater. And if she served a meal I did not like, I would end up just picking at it until she got tired of staring me down. Eventually she would order me to clear my plates off the table, reminding me that there won't be any more food for me since I did not eat what I'd been given. As a picky child, I could go all day without eating if I chose to, so I was not bothered by that threat. I remember my brother and I being afraid of her. We would always wonder when our parents would come to get us.

My grandmother liked to eat bitter kola and for some reason, one day she offered it to my brother and me. I had assumed it was merely an offer, so I declined, telling her I did not want it. I had never tasted it before but hearing the word bitter made me not want to. My brother, in a bid to avoid getting into trouble, took what she offered and ate it. I refused. I do not remember if she forced me to eat it or if she threatened me, but I remember eating the bitter kola and vomiting it all over my dress. It was a dress with frills that went across the front, and one of the frills caught most of the vomit, like a pocket. I remember her look of disgust as she ordered me out of her sight to get myself cleaned in the bathroom. I walked to the bathroom, unsure of what to do. I wasn't old enough to unzip my dress from behind, so I did not know what to do. I just stood in the bathroom with vomit on my dress. I'm not sure how long I stood there for, but a young guy came in and helped me get into clean clothes. I'd seen him around my grandparent's house a few times and assumed he was help of some sort. It was not until a year or two later that I understood that he was actually my uncle—my dad's youngest brother. He had probably been in his late teens or early twenties at the time.

As a child, I used to suck my thumb. I was usually able to resist the habit during the day, but at night, I would often tuck my thumb in between my lips and fall asleep that way. While we were visiting my grandparents, my grandmother would come into the room and pinch my thumb so hard I would feel the pain deep in my sleep and end up subconsciously moving my thumb out of my mouth. That was her mean way of getting me to stop sucking my thumb. Of course, that did not work, and I still sucked my thumb for a couple of years after that. I finally kicked the habit all on my own when I was eight. She must have somehow managed to pinch the exact spot on my thumb every night because I ended up with a scar there that remained for many years after that.

One morning, my brother and I woke up and found a little girl in my grandmother's house. She must have been three or so. She looked younger than we were. We watched in shock as she stepped on and jumped all over the sofa in my grandmother's house. Surely my grandmother would scold her or smack her as she did with us if we ever dared put our feet on her couch. But, no. My grandmother did not. I found out the little girl was my cousin who had just come with my aunty from the UK. I also met my aunty who had a British accent, which I thought was quite exotic since it was so foreign. Turns out that exotic flare garnered preferential treatment from my grandmother.

Fast-forward to two years after that, we had to live next to my grandmother for a few months. The way I understood it, my grandmother had built a house, and she had a spare apartment, so she had invited my dad to live in it for some reason. My mom had been against the idea and had ended up not coming with us. So, my dad moved into my grandmother's vacant three-bedroom apartment with my brother, my one-year-old sister, and me. He worked as a banker at the time and, due to the terrible traffic, he would always get home late at night, so I was responsible for my siblings while he was not home. My grandmother had insisted that after our chores and homework, we come to her apartment and sit for a few hours and then return to our apartment when it was time for bed. I am not sure about the reason for that. My brother and I did not like being around her, and she never seemed to want us around her either. When I think about it now, it just strikes me as her attempt at trying to control us.

Every evening my siblings and I would take the short one-minute walk to her apartment. While inside she would have us sit on the floor rather than on her sofa. The memory stuck with me because whenever my cousin visited from the UK, she was not treated like that. She was allowed to sit on the sofa and run around the house, making a lot of noise. Something we were not allowed to do. We always had to be quiet. My brother and I had a lot of inside jokes that we would whisper to each other. Whenever one of us burst out laughing, our grandmother would say, "Do share the joke." We knew better than to share the joke. We would just usually mutter, "Nothing." Usually she would let it go, but one day she insisted on hearing the joke.

My brother had pointed out to me that a scar on our grandmother's cheek looked like the top coating of a cooked custard after it had been left to cool. He was hesitant to share the joke but since she insisted, he told her what the joke was. She had been offended and twisted his ears and ended the twisting session with a smack to the back. I had also gotten an ear twist and a back slap for laughing at the joke. We never saw her raise her hands against her precious British granddaughter.

We ended up living close to her for about a year before moving out. A few years after, my parents once again took us to visit her for a brief day visit. My cousin was also there visiting from the UK with her younger brother who was about a year old at the time. At that time, I had another brother who was two or so. Suddenly my grandmother found some poop on her rug and pointed accusingly at my youngest sibling. I was thirteen years old and very defensive of all of my siblings. I told her I was sure my baby brother was not responsible because he was toilet trained. I even checked his underpants and there was no sign he had pooped. She refused to believe me and went on and on about it, asking me to clean it up. A short while later, my aunty found poop in other places around the house and discovered that her son's diaper had leaked. My grandmother did not apologize for the false accusation.

My grandmother also blamed my sister for breaking some contraption in her toilet sink even when she did not do it. We were happy when our parents came back to rescue us from the annoying visit. To this day, I do not understand why she treated us as inferior to our British cousins. We were not spoiled kids or troublesome in any way. We were actually very well behaved and disciplined. It seemed the only thing we did wrong was exist. She was known to be a very strict disciplinarian, but whenever the London cousins came to visit, she let a lot of their spoiled behavior slide and that was very obvious to me even as a young child; and even then I thought it was very unfair. *Were they somehow better than us because they were born in London and had British accents?*

This was in sharp contrast to how my other grandmother treated us—she was always pleasant and warm toward my siblings and me. She would always bring us Nigerian biscuits and soda from her shop each time we visited her and when she visited. We only got to visit with her twice a year while we were children. On Christmas Eve and on Easter, usually. She's in her nineties now, and although I didn't get to spend a lot of time with her growing up, some of my cousins did, and I can see how well they take care of her now. They would hug her and joke with her. To me, that meant she must have been a great and warm grandmother to them while they were growing up.

As of 2020, there are about 206 million people living in Nigeria. Lagos, the city I was born and raised in, has about 21 million people. I believe it's a good estimate that Black people make up 98% of Nigeria's population. Given my experience in the US, being a Black girl in a predominantly white country and state feels very different. Living in Nigeria, I gave no thought to my skin color. I was Black. That's who I was. That's who I am.

But yes, colorism is a thing even in Nigeria, just like in many parts of the world. Lighter-skinned Black people are considered more attractive, more beautiful. Some dark-skinned people choose to bleach their skins using harsh chemicals just because they want to be fairer, thinking that would make them more beautiful. Darker-skinned people were teased and called names like charcoal, shoe polish, night, shadow, and so on.

As a teenager, I saw this as harmless playground teasing as there was no violence involved, and I never saw or heard of anyone who was terribly bothered by this teasing. Of course, as an adult, I now realize that people can be bothered by teasing but choose not to let it show. And this is what often leads them down the path of skin bleaching. In all fairness, light-skinned people were also teased in the schoolyard. They were called *oyinbo*, fluorescent light. In fact, in Nigeria everyone got teased. You got teased if you were short, tall, fat, thin, rich, poor, and everything in between. Usually it's all harmless, friendly teasing.

I have never been the lightest or darkest in any random group of Nigerians, so I have never enjoyed any special treatment or attention for being light-skinned or teased for being dark. I've always been somewhere in the middle, and I've never been one to be bothered by my skin tone anyway.

Being Black in Nigeria is nothing like being Black in the US.

I came across a video clip involving two Black men that had gone viral. One of them was African and the other was American. In the video, the American man asked the African man why he was following him around the store. The African man said it was his job as a security officer to move around the store and observe the goings-on. The African man made it clear that it was silly that the Black American man would think the following was out of suspicion. The African man appeared nice and friendly in the video and even went on to call the American man his brother, saying he wouldn't he treat "his brother" in that way. The American seemed upset over a wrong he'd assumed was being done to him, saying the African was not his brother. Then the American added that the other man was not Black, but African.

Wait, what? Last time I checked, Africans are Black. *Of course, there are white Africans in South Africa and other non-Black Africans, but if you're clearly not white and you're obviously Black, why would anyone say you are not Black?* This an instance of trying to distinguish between their Blackness and someone else's.

Something I learned shortly after arriving to the US was that there is tension between many Africans and Black Americans. I've heard different theories about the source of this tension. Some say Black Americans dislike Africans for selling their own people into slavery out of greed and selfishness. Many Black Americans have ancestors who were slaves and feel that they are still experiencing the repercussions of slavery. Others say the dislike of Africans comes from Black Americans believing that Africans act like they are better than them, and that Africans think that the racism against Black Americans does not concern or affect them. I don't believe this is true. I've heard Nigerians say, "It doesn't matter if your name is Jayquan or Babatunde, all the white man sees is your black skin, and that's all they need to go by if they'll be racist toward you." So, Africans are definitely also concerned about racism.

I'm African and I don't see myself as better than Black Americans, or any other race for that matter. I also do not see myself as inferior to anyone from any race. We all have different life experiences and challenges, and we all have a choice in how we respond to these experiences and challenges.

The bottom line is that if we as Black people harbor prejudice against each other, what should we expect of other races?

Slavery was and is a terrible thing. The stories from that the early days of slavery are distressing to hear and read about. What's even more distressing is that these aren't mere stories but the realities that actual humans faced. I don't know if any of my ancestors participated in selling people into slavery, but even if they did it was not my fault. And I will not feel guilt or shame for something an ancestor of mine did. It was their choice to be greedy and evil. I should face the consequences of my own choices and decisions—not someone else's. All of the people involved in selling slaves in the 1700s are dead now. Although the consequences of their actions are still being felt to this day, no one should expect another to carry the guilt of something an ancestor they never knew did, however despicable.

It is very sad to think that there is still some form of slavery going on in these modern times. Modern-day slavery, as they call it. Children and adults are being sold into slavery and prostitution. This is happening in Africa, America, Europe, Asia— everywhere. I wish I had the superpower to bring down these modern-day slavery enterprises, destroy the perpetrators of this evil, and go back in time to stop slavery from ever happening. But I can't. The harm has been done and is still being done.

Unfortunately, to move toward a better future, I don't think there's one right answer. I feel like the best way forward is for everyone, regardless of race, to acknowledge the struggles of Black people. We all have to work together to help the Black community move forward, rather than constantly reminding them of their struggles or keeping them at a disadvantage. But it's a layered and complex problem to tackle.

Years ago, after I'd just arrived in the US, I learned about a slang used by some Nigerians to refer to Black Americans—*akata*. It's a word used to describe a stray wild cat, so in a sense when it's used, it points to the fact that Black Americans have no "home." I believe it's possible that some Africans might subconsciously look down on Black Americans. As Africans, we have a rich heritage and culture that we're very proud of. We know our roots. We can trace our lineage and ancestry and we're proud of those roots. Unfortunately, not all Black Americans know their roots, and that's likely a source of some of the bitterness they feel toward Africans. Some of Black Americans may feel that they were denied having roots because their ancestors were yanked from their homelands. Those ancestors had to fight to establish new roots and cultures among people who hated their guts and treated their animals better than they treated them.

Africans, on the other hand, love to showcase the pride we have for our cultures in the way we wear our hair, the kinds of fabrics we put on, our traditional weddings, and in so many aspects of our lives. I'm sure there are exceptions like I mentioned, but generally speaking, I don't think most Africans look down on Black Americans, some of whom prefer not to be called African Americans since they believe they don't all have African roots. I've never been a fan of those sorts of hyphenations anyway. I am Nigerian regardless of whether or not I am an American citizen, so I prefer not to be referred to as Nigerian-American. I find it a ridiculous way to alienate people, but maybe that's just me.

I digress. In reality, Africans are proud people. We are proud of who we are, we're proud of how far we've come—especially when we are able to thrive outside our home countries. I do think Africans can wonder why those who were born in the US, and who grew up in an environment we see as being better than the one we grew up in, don't do as well or even better than us. It can be disappointing to some Africans.

What we have to realize and understand as Africans is that we cannot buy into the stereotypes that have been painted about Black Americans. These are people who have gone through a lot.[3] Their ancestors were sold into slavery, raped, pillaged, murdered, treated worse than animals, and had to fight for their freedom. When they were freed, they had to fight for basic human rights. When we hear the word "ancestors," it often sounds like so long ago, but in reality, a few people who are grandchildren of slaves are still alive today. Some of those who fought for human and civil rights are also still alive today to tell firsthand stories.

After slaves were declared free in 1863, they attempted establish their own roots. They owned thriving businesses, had properties, and built wealth over the course of five decades. But they lost all of it. In 1921, a mob of white people burned, and looted houses and businesses owned by Black people in Tulsa, Oklahoma.[4] This racial violence rendered more than 8,000 people homeless. Nearly two years after that, another racially motivated massacre occurred in Florida where a predominantly Black town, Rosewood, Florida, was burned to the ground by a white mob.[5] Churches were burned down, homes were burned down, and Black people were murdered. These are just few of the many race wars that Black people have faced over the years, and the resulting homelessness, loss of loved ones, and hopelessness has taken and continues to take a toll on the Black community.

Those examples are just a few examples of the systemic racism and injustices that have been integral parts of America since its foundation. These injustices plague the Black community. After decades of ill treatment and being beaten down, it appears that both the political system and the justice system are rigged against Black folks. Even as many Black people try to move on, they are striving to overcome the psychological warfare that has stood against them for decades and continues today. Being told they are not good enough, are inferior, are not worthy to occupy the same space as others, do not belong in a country that their ancestors built with their blood, sweat, and tears, are not worth investing in, do not deserve to live—these are damaging and enduring psychological scars.

On the other hand, I've heard many Black Americans discriminate against African immigrants. I have African immigrant friends who describe their experience with discrimination at the hands of Black Americans. One of the things Black Americans say about African immigrants is that "they have come to take our jobs." My questions are: "What jobs? The ones you did not have before we came into the country? How can we 'take' something we worked very hard for? Mind you, many African immigrants came into the country with at least a bachelor's degree. Many worked hard to get a master's degree and a doctorate degree while in America, so of course when a job opportunity comes along that they are qualified for, they will apply for it. If things work out, they get these jobs." There is a lot that can be said about what African immigrants go through to become established in the US, and I believe this argument of any immigrant coming to take or steal jobs is one of ignorance born out of poverty.

All that said, we all co-exist with the American system. Immigrants often have more in common with the plight of Black Americans, especially those of us from Africa. We have endured a lot of psychological torture from our own governments. These governments have consistently placed their greed above their needs. And look how most of the population has turned out. There's a lot of hopelessness, despair, and crime. I believe even as we've taken the bold step to leave hopelessness and despair behind, we must advocate for our Black American brothers and sisters however we can.

SANITY VS. INSANITY

I'D JUST COUNSELED AN ELDERLY white male on a vaccine when he asked me, "Are you from the one of the Caribbean islands?"

I replied no, not volunteering any more information.

"I detect a familiar accent," he pressed.

"I'm from Nigeria," I replied.

He continued, "Are you from Lagos?" Usually when an American says that to me, they have either visited Lagos or lived there for a bit.

I replied yes.

He smiled and said he lived in Lagos for a few years, and the last time he was there was 1999. He'd worked in the US embassy there. He added that he'd worked in the US embassy in Cameroon and some other parts of Africa too. I nodded and said I thought that was interesting.

He then said, "I have one question for you."

I nodded, encouraging him to go ahead.

He said, "Why are Nigerians so smart?"

I chuckled. The question caught me off guard. I shrugged, "Maybe because we have to cope with a lot of hardship and stress in Nigeria, so when we leave for developed countries we end up thriving because the environment there is easier, and we don't feel like we are constantly fighting a system that doesn't have our best interest at heart."

Life in Nigeria is something I cannot forget. It's still very vivid in my mind even nearly six years after leaving.

The dusty roads had me constantly sneezing due to severe allergies. With my atopic genes, I had daily struggles with dust-induced allergies and asthma. I always had several handkerchiefs with me to cover my nose with when I could. Electricity was something we never came to expect. Almost everyone had a generator in their home. Nights were so noisy from the sound of all the generators coming out to play. We invented new ways to iron our clothes without electricity.

One of the first things we hear in Nigeria about Western countries is "they never take the light" which means there is power supply 24/7. Anytime we experience uninterrupted power supply for more than twenty-four hours, we would start to panic. It was almost always a bad omen because that sort of uninterrupted power supply usually preceded weeks to months of no power supply. We would always make sure phones were fully charged, work clothes and school uniforms were all ironed days in advance, and rechargeable lamps were fully charged. Like a self-fulfilling prophecy, after the second or third day of uninterrupted power supply, we more often than not wouldn't have power for the next few weeks. And if by some cruel twist of fate, there also happens to be nationwide fuel scarcity, which is a frequent occurrence in Nigeria, around the time where power supply has been paused for an indeterminable period of time, we end up being plunged into nightly darkness since we need fuel to power our backup generators.

As if the country's dire situation isn't bad enough, we have to deal with harassment by police officers and soldiers. We have to choose between being morally upright citizens who don't offer bribes, and getting home in one piece without spending the whole day in their custody, accused of some fabricated crime.

The majority of the policemen in Nigeria are corrupt, and they are the bane of motorists' existence. With all the anger many Nigerians have toward police officers, we would choose them over Nigerian soldiers. Soldiers are a ruthless, merciless, and heartless bunch. An example of how ruthless they can be is that they do not allow civilians to put on any item of clothing that closely resembles camouflage. There is no law that prohibits Nigerian citizens from wearing camouflage, but apparently no one sent that memo to Nigerian soldiers. They have written their own handbook on how no one else other than members of the Nigerian Army are allowed to put on camouflage. There have been numerous reports of them ordering civilians to strip down to their underwear in public because they had camouflage pants on. How humiliating! As much as we have a general dislike and distrust of policemen and soldiers in Nigeria, seeing both of them get into fights—many times violent—over who has more authority is a source of entertainment for tired, drained Nigerians trying to get home after an exhausting day, a good portion of which has been spent sitting in traffic for hours.

Meanwhile in America, when people see soldiers, they thank them for their service and for their sacrifice. Some even offer them free meals at restaurants. I'm not saying Nigerian soldiers don't risk their lives or sacrifice a lot to protect the country. I'm sure they do. My issue with them is why they see the need to terrorize the same citizens they are supposed to be protecting, especially over something as trivial as a style of clothing. Just because it's similar to a soldier's uniform does not mean no one else can wear it. Perhaps they get their sense of worth as soldiers from their uniform rather than from their skills.

It's sad that as a country, Nigeria doesn't learn from past mistakes. We continue to elect the same corrupt leaders that have led us down the path of misery in the past. One of the allures of Western countries is that their systems work. You pay taxes, and you see the results of those taxes. Roads are being constructed and repaired. Electricity works if you pay for it. There are often welfare systems in place. There are laws to guide how people ought to behave and not even the law enforcement agencies *should be* above the law. The legal system may not always be fair and just, but at least they try to follow protocol as best as they can. In countries like the US and Canada, there is freedom of speech. The US president is not above the law and should not be. Elections are transparent and fair, for the most part.

It's the opposite in Nigeria and many parts of Africa. Nothing works in Nigeria. There is a lot of madness that goes on there. I grew up in the western part of Nigeria in a city with about 21 million people. Lagos is a hub of activity. People come from all over the country hoping that by moving to Lagos, they would be able to catch a break. This is similar to young artists in America moving to Los Angeles in the hopes of catching a lucky break. Some succeed, some don't.

I wish African youth were concerned about more important things rather than what country's jollof rice is best. It's Nigerian jollof rice, by the way.

We Nigerians have a saying that if we can survive in Nigeria, then we can survive anywhere else. Air-conditioning, power supply, and good roads are luxuries rather than basic necessities. And a required national volunteer program tests our survival skills even further.

I had to volunteer in another part of Nigeria after I graduated from university. It is a requirement that every Nigerian graduate serve the country by participating in a scheme called the National Youth Service Corps (NYSC), also known as National Service. This, to me, is one of the many ridiculous and irrelevant laws still being observed in Nigeria. Its aim is to foster unity among the different ethnic groups in Nigeria by allowing young graduates to live among people of other ethnic origins so as to appreciate their culture. Participating in the NYSC is a requirement in order to be employed by a government-owned organization in Nigeria. Are there people who did not participate but found jobs in government-owned organizations? Yes, but it usually involves a lot of palm greasing and "inside connections," as we call them.

The way the NYSC works is this. Universities send out the names of all the graduating students each year to the government, which in turn sends back the list of names with their assigned NYSC locations. What they try to do is not assign people from a particular state to that same state. The reasoning behind that is to foster unity among various tribes and cultures since Nigeria is very large and is home to three hundred seventy-one tribes and about five hundred languages. So, if you're originally from Lagos, you won't be deployed to serve in Lagos, you'll be deployed to serve in a different state. Sure, people who do not want to leave their home state find a way to bribe and worm their way out of being deployed outside their states. It's a year-long deployment with an initial three-week orientation at a campground in the assigned state.

I hated every minute of those three weeks. I was posted to Edo state. I had never lived outside of Lagos before, so it was interesting to me to be living in another state. That interest was very short-lived, though. We had to wear uniforms while on the camp. The only time we were allowed to wear mufti (plain clothes) was when we walked through the camp gates for the first time. After that, we were required to change into white t-shirts, white shorts, white socks, and white tennis shoes.

The camp was run by military men and women, and we were expected to obey their every command. The rooms were large halls filled with about two hundred bunk beds with barely enough room to move. There was no running water, no flushable toilets—there were only pit latrines available, and the bathrooms had no doors. I looked around and sighed, thinking, *What kind of life is this?* But like everything else in Nigeria, we just have to adapt to it. I remember there being an option of either trekking some distance to get water or paying someone to do so. I also remember there being a few teenagers going around asking if they could be of service to either do laundry or fetch water for anyone interested. I found someone who I paid to get water for me daily. I would "buy" three buckets of water for bathing and washing my clothes. We all had to wear white, on a very dusty campground, under scorching heat. There was certainly a need for daily washing of those whites.

One major problem with having hundreds to a thousand people living on a campground is theft. From time to time, there would be someone crying over their money that was just stolen, while raining curses on whoever stole their money. I kept my money in a belly pouch we were allowed to wear on our uniform and slept with it under my pillow and with the straps wrapped around my hand. The rest of my stuff was in a bag beneath the bunk bed, padlocked shut. There were cases of people stealing other people's buckets of water. Luckily, no one stole mine.

Those of us who were in health-related professions enjoyed a bit of special treatment. There was a camp clinic in the center of camp where pharmacists, nurses, and doctors were told to convene, and we were given the task of caring for the health of the camp residents. That was a good escape from many camp activities. At 5 a.m. every morning, the soldiers would come banging rudely on the room doors to wake everyone up. If no one stirred, they would storm in and begin yelling into people's ears. There was a required 5 a.m. assembly where we would switch from singing Christian worship songs to yelling military chants. Then by 6 a.m., we would start the morning drills and workouts. After that, the day would start with various activities. It was exhausting.

They served breakfast, lunch, and dinner at the camp kitchen. Mealtimes always involved getting in very long lines, holding your plate, and having someone slap a spoon of something into it when it got to your turn. I tried the food for the first two days, and I was done with it. I found it very unappealing. There was a market called Mami Market within the camp where all sorts of things were sold, including snacks, food, and drinks. I would buy one meal at Mami market and be all set for the day. On Sundays, I would eat the food from the kitchen because it was jollof rice day, and it was the only thing they served from that kitchen that I could actually eat. I was very careful with what I ate, though. I hated using the pit latrine. I remember pooping only three times in three weeks. The thought of the pit latrine buzzing with huge flies was enough to seal up my bowels for a week at a time. After a week of so many humans being on the campground, the place was disgusting. Especially the bathroom areas which faced the entrance to the halls where we slept. The floors were muddy from people bathing outside. The bathroom stalls were not enough for everyone to bathe in at a time, and there were always those people that refused to wait till a stall became available. Then there were those disgusting human beings who would refuse to defecate in the pit latrines and would do it in a plastic bag and throw it over the fence.

A good number of people managed to get themselves transferred out of Edo state back to Lagos, using made-up medical conditions as the reason. I suffer from asthma from time to time, and asthma was one of the conditions people would claim just to be posted back to their home states. People would say that they "needed to be close to their doctor who is in so-so state due to how severe their asthma attacks can get." Many of those people did not even know what asthma was. Some even got doctors to write up false medical diagnoses as proof of their need to be transferred back to their states of origin. With the campground being very dusty, I had my inhaler with me all the time. A few people in the clinic saw me with my inhaler and asked why I had not requested a transfer back to Lagos. My asthma was not that severe, and I did not want to have a doctor embellish the truth for my sake.

After a week working in the clinic, I found out that we could actually sleep in one of the beds in there, so I began to do that instead of beginning the short trek back to the crowded halls to share sleeping space with hundreds of people. I was one of the pharmacists in charge of dispensing medications. I ran a tight ship since we had limited supply, and the soldiers had told us there was no more supply coming in. We had to manage with what we had. When the doctors prescribed an antibiotic, I would suggest an alternative that the patient would actually adhere to, and I would have the patients come in daily to take their meds under my watchful gaze to avoid pill sharing and patients not completing their antibiotic therapy. I quickly gained a reputation for being strict.

I was glad when the three-week camp orientation was over. On the last day, we had to dress up in the NYSC outfit consisting of a white, crested vest, green khaki pants, yellow boots, topped with a green cap. There was a "passing-out" ceremony to celebrate the end of camp, and people either went back to their home state or went to the new jobs they were posted to within the service state. It was a few days before Easter, but I decided to continue on to the rural town I was posted to work in to get my work assignment squared away before heading back to Lagos for Easter.

My assigned town was a very rural and unremarkable. I had the bus drop me off at the teaching hospital I was assigned to. I went to the Human Resources office to introduce myself and get all the paperwork started. They let me know they were already winding down due to the Easter holiday approaching, so I would not be able to complete any paperwork till after the holiday. It felt like a wasted journey. Perhaps I should have just headed back to Lagos from the camp instead of taking a one-hour bus ride into the town. Frustrated, I walked outside of the hospital gate and flagged down a motorcycle. I grew up viewing motorcycles as one of many modes of public transportation in Lagos, but in this rural town, they were one of two modes of transportation—unmarked taxis or cabs. I had no leads on housing or how anything worked in that area, so when the motorcycle rider stopped in front of me, I said, "Take me to the nearest hotel." He could see I was a "corper," as we were called, from my NYSC uniform, and he asked where I was from. I told him Lagos. He said he'd visited Lagos before. He took me to a hotel and said I could call him whenever I needed a ride. I thanked him and checked into the hotel.

After resting in the hotel room for a few minutes, I called the front desk to see if I could order some room service. I was told there was no food to order and that their kitchen was closed. *Sigh.* I asked how I could get food. They could arrange to have someone go into town to get me some food, the front desk person told me. I agreed and had food delivered shortly. I was exhausted and felt very drained from the past couple of weeks. It had been a seven-hour bus ride to the camp from Lagos. And after being under the scorching sun, doing early morning drills, being yelled at by military men, caring for sick corps members for three weeks, enduring an hour-long, rickety bus ride to the town, I was exhausted.

I felt very alone for the first time in my life. Everything and everyone I knew was in Lagos. In retrospect, that year-long stay in that rural town prepared me for living thousands of miles away from everything and everyone I know. I remember the feeling of loneliness the first few months I lived in Boston, but I embraced the loneliness, knowing it would be temporary. Before long I made a few friends in school and in church, and I began to feel less alone.

Having lived in a place like Lagos, not a lot fazes me about American life. Much of what I described from Nigeria may seem insane to many. But dealing with those challenges my whole life prepared me to find sanity in spite of life disruptions. I remember one day in the summer of 2017, the power had gone out in the city where my husband and I lived. That was my first experience with power outage in the US, and I was amused. This was a constant feature in life in Nigeria so I was not bothered by it. I assumed it won't be out for too long and certainly not for days on end like in Nigeria. I figured there had to be a reason for the outage and not just an attempt to ration electricity like in my home country.

The power did not come back on even after a few hours. I was studying for my Pharmacy Boards at the time, but since we had a battery-powered torchlight, I used that as a light source for my reading. After a few hours, I realized there was reason to be bothered. We had a lot of food in the freezer. If the power outage went on for too long, they would thaw and be ruined. The stove was powered by electricity so there was no hope of cooking anything. I realized that modern, urban America is not really set up for power outages.

In Nigeria we were not bothered by power outages because our daily lives could very well go on without electricity.

The night of my first American power outage, we opened the windows and went to bed without electricity. By the time we woke up in the morning, the power was restored. Admittedly if that had happened during the winter, I wouldn't have been more bothered by the power outage because heat is a priority for me during the winter. Northeastern winters are their own type of insanity.

YOU SPEAK GOOD ENGLISH FOR A NIGERIAN

AS A NIGERIAN, I KNOW I am not alone when I say I cannot count how many times an American has uttered these very words to me. Words which, to me, expose their ignorance, but to them is probably meant as a…compliment? "Wow, you speak very good English."

I've had people say to me, "I hear an accent. I love accents! Don't tell me. Let me guess where you're from." And we turn it into a game of "No, I'm not from Jamaica."

I find that amusing, really. If someone is intrigued or curious about a foreigner's accent, it's okay to be friendly and ask them about it directly. I've never felt offended over being asked where my accent is from, or what country I'm from. If it's odd to tell an American that they speak good English, then it's odd to say that to a non-American.

Some have even tried to justify my ability to speak comprehensible English by asking how long I've lived in the US. One time, I replied, "Two years." The woman's response was "Wow, you must be a fast learner!" Sigh.

Sometimes I don't even bother correcting them and letting them know that English is my first language.

In Nigeria, more than five hundred languages are spoken. I do not understand all five hundred languages. The average Nigerian is fluent in at least one of these five hundred languages. Some are fluent in more than one, and those people usually conduct business in states other than their native states, or in cities where people who are from different tribes and/or who speak different dialects converge to do business or to live.

English is the official language of Nigeria and helps us to communicate with each other despite language differences. English is the medium of communication in schools and organizations all over the country. Due to illiteracy, some people never get to learn how to speak English, and we have to resort to pidgin English to communicate. Although, there are many literate people who prefer to speak pidgin English within their circle of friends even if they are all literate and are proficient in English. They see it as more informal, and they claim that it rolls off the tongue like poetry.

I was giving an elderly white man a vaccine one day when he said to me, "Parlez-vous Francais?" I understood that because I had taken three years of French in secondary school and understood beginner level French. I told him no, and after that he said, "Oh, you're not from the part of Africa that speaks French, then?" He told me briefly about his travels and how he was learning Dutch at seventy-something years old. He liked to travel often to Germany to visit friends, and although his friends were fluent in English, they enjoyed communicating in their native Dutch language. He wanted to be able to join them in conversation.

I'm always glad to hear things like that. It is great to want to share in other people's cultures. Immigration brings a lot of color and flavor to any country, and those who resist it lose out on the richness that is found in the blending of cultures.

Depending on my mood, my response to being told that I speak good English ranges anywhere from a polite smile to "I have been speaking English since I learned how to talk" to "I probably speak better English than you."

I encountered someone whom I was counseling about the side effects of a medication who said to me, "Wow, your English is very good." I am not always in the best of moods when I'm at work since it's such a stressful environment, so I replied, "Yes, we speak English in Nigeria." He had a sheepish look on his face and looked like he was not sure whether to apologize or not.

The ignorance about Nigerians speaking proficient English is equally annoying in the university context. Most US universities require us to take the Test of English as a Foreign Language (TOEFL) or the International English Language Testing System (IELTS) to prove that we understand English enough to communicate and understand lectures in American schools. First of all, many of us were taught in English back in our home countries. It would be more reasonable to require only students from primarily non-English-speaking countries to take these tests. It is very easy to make a distinction between English-speaking and non-English-speaking countries. I remember applying to a few universities in Canada who classified Nigeria and other countries in Africa which were colonized by the British as English-speaking; that exempted us from taking an English test to prove our proficiency.

The TOEFL contains different sections on reading, listening, speaking, and writing. It takes about three hours total. I had to take it twice. Once in Nigeria as one of the requirements for graduate school application, and again in the US as a second step in the foreign pharmacy graduate equivalency process, the other requirement being passing the foreign pharmacy equivalency examination. If I could pass the actual equivalency exam that tests my foreign pharmacy education, shouldn't that tell them I was able to understand English? Needless to say, I had a perfect score on each section. The irony is that a good number of so-called native English speakers would not be able to pass all those sections on the exam. I've heard a few Americans say they hated English as a subject in school. I loved learning English, especially in secondary school. I loved the teacher I had. I loved writing essays and I loved those random, unexpected dictation exercises she would give us in class.

I imagine many so-called native English speakers that would fail the TOEFL writing section are those that use *your* instead of *you're*, *there* when they mean *their*, and *could of* instead of *could have*. The list is endless! Not to be a grammar policewoman, but how hard is it to get these words straight?

I was on an online dating site once, and on my About Me section I added: "Please don't message me if you don't know the difference between there vs their, your vs you're." Some people on the site found that funny, others not so much. I think we know what category those who didn't find it funny belong to.

I once knew an American girl who pronounced the word comfortable as "contable." It took me a while to figure out what she was saying until I finally pieced it together from context. It was the oddest thing.

I've continued studying Spanish, and I practiced it with my housemates in grad school. To me, learning multiple languages opens up one's mind to other cultures. When you know how to speak a language other than your native language, you'll be more eager and comfortable visiting that country. You'll also be more excited to meet people who speak that language.

It takes a one-minute Google search to figure out the primary language of different countries, but if one is so curious, it's okay to just ask: "What language do you speak in your home country?" You never know what kind of relationship you can strike up.

THE THIEF OF GRATITUDE

I WAS THIRTEEN OR SO when I came home and told my mom I wanted a new school bag. She looked at my school bag and asked what was wrong with it. "It is old!" I complained bitterly. My mom looked at me and pointed out that it was still in good condition. I told her how my friends brought new school bags to school every new term, and I hated having to bring the same bag to school term after term, year after year. My mom made me understand that she had spent a little more than usual on our school bags because she knew they would last for a long time. She made it clear that she was not going to spend her money on lower quality bags that would need replacing after a few months of use and that she was not going to replace bags that were in perfect condition. She added that she was sure there were also other kids in my class and school that did not change their bags every term either because they had practical parents like her, or because they could not afford to even if their bags were in poor condition.

Thirteen-year-old me was not too impressed with her practicality. My parents worked hard to provide us with all we needed, not necessarily all we wanted. As a teenager, I understood that asking my parents to buy me something just because I saw someone else with that thing was a lost cause. If I could show the necessity of having that thing, then I was more likely to get it. If my reason for wanting it was because someone else had it, then I would most definitely *not* be getting it. This taught me to really focus less on what people had that I did not, knowing that if I needed it, I could get it. As a teenager, I had enough wisdom to know when I really needed something and when I merely wanted it for the sake of having it. That wisdom has guided me throughout my adult life.

It's so easy to fall into the trap of comparison but, unfortunately, nothing good comes out of comparing oneself to someone else. Comparison and admiration are two different things. It's fine to admire someone who's doing something phenomenal or exemplary. It is understandable to want to follow in the footsteps of someone who's doing remarkable things. Admiration brings inspiration and often helps us identify our passion and find our own paths.

Comparison, on the other hand, is a thief of contentment and gratitude. Comparison makes us forget the major milestones we have reached, the great feats we have accomplished, the wonderful things we have been blessed with. Instead, it keeps us focused on the things other people have that we don't. I can't think of anything else that can instill bitterness in a person's heart more easily than comparing your current status to someone else's. Life is filled with so many different calibers and classes of people. Change, as we know, is a constant in life. Another constant in life that is not so commonly talked about is the difference in social class and status among humans. There will always be people who have more than you have at any given point just as there will always be people who have less than you do.

Luckily, as I passed through my teenage phase, I observed other kids in school whose parents couldn't afford what mine could. So, I learned to appreciate all I was blessed with and was never the sort to envy what other people had. As I got into college, I grew even more secure and content with all I had. I didn't try to be like anyone else or covet what others had. I had dreams and desires for the future, and my mind was filled with things I wanted to achieve. I admired people who were where I wanted to be or had things I hoped to have in the future. To me, they were a source of encouragement rather than a source of comparison and envy. I realize that's one of my strengths, and not everyone is as strong in this area.

Here's how my mind works. The only time I ever would justify comparing myself to someone else is if they were born on the exact day and time I was, had identical life experiences to mine, had the same opportunities I had, experienced the same challenges I did, and pretty much are living my life, just in a different body. I have yet to meet such a person, so I really can't justify comparing myself to anyone else. I am always baffled when someone starts to feel inferior or insecure over something or someone they saw on social media. Social media is the worst place to find someone to compare oneself with. Nothing is ever as it seems on social media, and nobody's life is perfect, however well they paint it to be so.

I recently worked with three young pharmacy technicians who asked me what age I was when I got married and when I had my first child. I told them I was twenty-seven when I got married and twenty-nine when I had my first child. They seemed to find some comfort in my response.

One of them had just broken off a five-year relationship she had been hoping would lead to marriage. She felt that she had just wasted the last five years of her life. She was only twenty-two at the time. I don't understand the rush for marriage at that age because in my opinion, there is a lot more she could be doing with her life. She admitted that she had been seeing a lot of posts on social media by girls her age showing them either getting married, getting pregnant, or having babies. She also admitted that she felt inadequate because she was not doing any of those things. I assured her that she was in no way inadequate just because she isn't married or pregnant at twenty-two. I asked her if she would rather rush into marriage now and end up miserable or wait patiently to meet the right man even if it meant getting married later than she wanted to, if that meant long-lasting peace.

I'm not implying that those who rush into marriage always end up miserable. But more often than not, those who rush into marriages or rush to have children because they feel pressured by society, social media, family members, or even their own feelings of inadequacy end up with regrets. After you have that husband and that baby that you felt pressured to have, what then? There will always be more pressure—there's always more that you feel pressed to do because everyone else around you is doing the same. Keeping up with the Joneses is a never-ending race.

I did my best to encourage those young girls and reassure them that there was so much they could be doing until they personally feel ready to make a marriage commitment. I forgot how loud my voice can get when I'm speaking about something I'm very passionate about until one of the clerks at the front of the store rushed to the pharmacy to check if everything was alright. He said it sounded like there was a fight going on when he heard voices raised. We assured him we were just got carried away with our discussion. I still get teased about that episode whenever I visit that pharmacy.

I've discovered that I have a passion for encouraging young girls and letting them know it's okay to be your own person and to have a mind of your own. It's okay to not be ready to be married at twenty-three or twenty-five or thirty. It's okay to find joy in dreaming about a certain career or business. It is okay to stand out from the crowd. It is okay to abstain from sex until marriage if that's what you choose in your heart to do. It's okay not to sleep around even if everyone around you is. It's okay not to have a boyfriend even if you're the only single one in your group of friends. It's okay not to do what it seems everyone else is doing. It's okay to stay off social media if that's a source of comparison and envy for you. It's perfectly okay to choose your own path. It's also okay to choose to be married at any age as long as it is *you* who's doing the choosing and not society or social media expectations.

There is a lot of peace and contentment that comes from living life on one's terms. I get pretty worked up when I hear young girls consider letting their dreams and aspirations die because they feel inadequate from seeing what other people are doing.

As an immigrant, one could be tempted to compare oneself to other immigrants.

We arrived in America the same year, why is she doing better than I am?

She has bought a house already? But I came to this country before her!

He is sending a lot of money back home, and I can barely meet up with my bills.

She got the job of her dreams, and I'm still stuck with this job I hate so much. I'm pretty sure I work harder than she does.

It never ends. There is always something to be envious of if we let ourselves. It's little wonder that the rate of depression has increased in the past couple of years. And I don't think it's a coincidence that social media use among youths has also increased over that time. While some scientific studies have observed a link between depression and the volume of social media use, others claim there is no direct correlation.[6,7]

Still, other than those who have suffered painful losses or experienced a negative life event, the root cause of many cases of depression in people is comparison. Comparing oneself with someone else without knowing their story or how they struggled to get to where they are is never a good idea. *Why would I compare myself with someone who's stunting on social media with money they got from running illegal businesses, dancing in strip clubs, selling their bodies, or doing things I would never do? Why would I compare myself to someone who has worked very hard to achieve what they have and is years ahead of me when I have not had to work as hard or had the benefit of the years of labor they have put in?* I don't see any basis for comparison in any scenario.

In all honesty, I believe that having faith in God and having a relationship with Him is the key to the kind of peace, joy, and contentment that we all seek. This is the only kind of peace and contentment that helps us to battle the depression and anxiety that appears to be a major part of life on earth.

In my own little way, I tried to encourage those young technicians to follow their dreams of higher education and a fulfilling career. Everything else will fall into place if it's meant to be. I said something that resonated with me long after my shift ended that day.

"I am exactly where I want to be in my life right now," I said matter-of-factly to the girls, and I meant it.

On my drive home that night, I gave it more thought. *Am I really?* And my answer to myself in the quiet of my car was a resounding yes.

I certainly aspire to do more things with my life. I would love to sponsor at least one underprivileged child through undergraduate school. I would love to adopt at least one child. I would love to be able to donate a lot of money to charities. I would love to build an orphanage in Nigeria. There is so much I feel called to do, yet I am perfectly content with exactly where I am in life right now. I have come so far—from the fresh-faced international student living in Boston, to the recent graduate hoping to land a job to pay off her loans quickly, to the intern studying hard into the night to pass her Pharmacy Boards, to the pharmacist who worked hard and deprived herself of luxury to pay off all her loans and start a nonprofit. It's been quite a wild ride. I did not go through half of the things some immigrants went through to settle in this country, and I'm sure I went through more challenges than others. I have everything I need if not everything I want, and I am content.

Yes, I am exactly where I want to be, and I would not change anything for all the oil in the Middle East.

STRANGER THAN STRANGE

I FELL OUT OF A moving vehicle when I was about six years old. I had been sleeping and resting on the door, without a seatbelt on, when the door flung open as my dad took a sharp turn. Needless to say, I was rudely awakened from my early evening nap.

I was sitting on the passenger side, which used to be my best seat in the car as a child. The fall and the noise from the market women behind me yelling for the car to stop, had me feeling like I was in a weird dream. I saw my dad running toward me in shock. It was a busy road, usually but somehow that day no car had been coming behind us. At least I don't remember there being any.

He scooped me up and jogged back toward the car. There was a large bleeding bruise on the back of my thigh, and I was in pain. I ended up spending a week or so in the hospital. Ever since, the first thing my dad would say when any of us got into the car was "seatbelts, please!"

I imagine that if such a thing were to happen here in the US, Child Protective Services would have been called. One can't even spank one's child in public without people staring judgingly at the parent. Growing up in Nigeria, spanking a child, to me, was as normal as eating three square meals. Nearly every parent spanked their kids. Parents who let their child run around screaming and throwing tantrums in public, without spanking them right there, were seen as careless and terrible. People would look at the mother and shake their heads in disappointment. Some would even go the extra mile and tell her to spank the child, declaring that as the best way to train a child. School teachers were even allowed to hit students with canes. Canes used by teachers in Nigeria—and I assume many parts in Africa—are long, thin sticks, usually made from rattan. They range anywhere from two feet to four feet long. Caning is very common as a form of corporal punishment in Nigerian schools. Between being caned in school and spanked at home, it was easy to get used to the idea of spanking as the only form of discipline as an African child. A popular quote among Nigerian parents who were advocates of spanking was: "Spare the rod and spoil the child."

As someone who has been slapped so hard I literally saw stars, I have never agreed with violent spanking as the only way to discipline a child, even as a teenager. It seemed that as soon as I finished secondary school, I somehow graduated from spanking.

I won't forget the day a neighbor, who happened to be a receptionist in my secondary school, dropped by our house one night when my mom had just returned from work. She was a busybody, that woman. She had stopped me earlier that day in school while walking with some of my friends and questioned why I had lip gloss on. I cannot remember what my response to her had been, but it would have been a typical response of a fifteen-year-old being asked to clean off her lip gloss in front of her friends. How embarrassing! I had also gone out of school with some friends during break time for ice cream. Apparently she had seen me doing so, and she had come to report me to my mother.

I remember this day very well because I saw stars for a day after getting slapped. That became a reality for me and not just a figure of speech. As soon as the receptionist came in and told my mom she had come to report something I did at school, my mom called for me to be present. I sat on the arms of two sofas that had been pushed close together and listened to her narrate how I went out of school with some friends, and how I had on lip gloss and was rude to her when she had asked me to rub it off. She added that she was just concerned I was starting to move with the wrong friends. I was furious. *How did going out for ice cream constitute moving with wrong friends?* Going out of school during break time was not wrong. It was permitted. And even though my mom did not let me have or use lip gloss, I did not think there was anything wrong with trying on my friend's pink-tinted lip gloss. I had a mental image of diving toward her, my arms reaching for her neck.

After her report, my mom turned to me and said, "Ngbọ́?" which is Yoruba for "Is that true?"

All I managed to say was, "Um—" when my mom backhanded me across the face. I thought I had gone blind for a second because the room had been dark, with only a kerosene lantern on for illumination. Yet I saw bright lights flash for a brief moment. I did not listen to any of what my mom yelled since I was busy trying to blink to make sure my eyes still worked well. The nosy woman left. I've hated her ever since, and she knew it. Each time I saw her in school I would shoot daggers at her with my eyes.

Living in Nigeria, one of the things we would hear from Nigerians who lived abroad was that they could not spank their children. They described British and American children calling the cops on their parents if they ever dared to spank them. I always thought those stories were exaggerated until I lived in the US.

I was surprised to learn that some parents never spank their children. I reasoned that as long as they were able to discipline them in other ways there was nothing wrong with that. Spanking and discipline don't have to go hand in hand. They are not mutually exclusive, although to the average Nigerian and, dare I say, African parent, they are. What baffles me is that there actually exist parents who do not discipline their children at all. They raise spoiled, rotten children with no form of home training and unleash them into the world. Baffling.

While living in Boston, I had a housemate who told me she did not want to have children. She hoped to be married someday but had no desire to have kids. She said she loved kids and she looked forward to being a fun aunt to her future nieces and nephews, and even my own future kids. I wanted to know why she didn't want kids of her own. I thought, *Why would any female who is married not want to have children barring any fertility issues? That's so American.*

But then it dawned on me that I have been raised to think a certain way for so long that I had never considered that there is more than one right way to go about life. Since my early days as an immigrant, I've come to understand and agree that everyone has the right to think for themselves outside of culture and set traditions. Contrary to what many African societies believe, yes, it's perfectly okay for a woman or man to not have a desire to be married, and for a married couple to decide not to have any children. Many Africans believe there is some witchcraft or spiritual force at play when they hear things like that, but there are a lot of factors that influence such choices, which we are not privy to (not that it's anyone's business), which has nothing to do with the supernatural. The bottom line is that there is absolutely nothing wrong with those kinds of choices. Just like there is nothing wrong with the way people choose to raise their children as long as they grow up to be decent, disciplined, sensible adults.

I wish many Americans loved their fellow human beings as much as they love their pets. I have never seen anyone treat pets the way Americans do. They carry them in their handbags, allow them to sleep in the same bed with them, and worst of all, they kiss them on their mouths and allow them to lick their mouths. In Nigeria, pets stay outside the house. They are free to roam about within the compound at night and during the day. But if they are wild dogs, they are kept in a kennel when visitors come around to prevent them from attacking them. Wild dogs are for guarding the property usually and not necessarily pets to be played with or allowed on one's bed. The local dogs are the friendly ones and are seen roaming around on the streets, some without owners. Many residents found this annoying and asked dog owners to keep their dogs in their own compounds.

Dogs aren't maltreated where I'm from, but they aren't given special treatments either. They eat the same meals as members of the household. In fact, they are sometimes included in the spanking when they misbehave just like anyone else. I realize some people will consider spanking a dog as maltreatment. There is actually a tribe in Nigeria that eats dog meat as part of their cultural delicacy just like people eat beef, lamb, chicken, and so on, but I won't talk about that here. I've observed over the years that some people would take their dogs to dog daycares, for dog massages and dog spa sessions, but will not raise a helping hand to another human who is genuinely in need. I mean, if you can pick up your dog's feces from the road, the least you can do is treat another human with respect and kindness. *Why should an animal be getting better treatment than a human?*

Cats are a whole different matter. Nigerians in general hate cats. Black cats, in particular. There is a superstition that cats are evil because witches often metamorphose into cats. So, cats are related to the occult and are not to be trusted or allowed into one's yard. I remember silent whispers of "blood of Jesus" each time people come into contact with cats on the street or if one gets into their yard. I never believed the superstition, but somehow deep down in my subconscious, I developed a wariness of cats.

I remember being in Miami on vacation with my friend, Malo. We rented an Airbnb and although the owner mentioned that she had cats, I had wrongly assumed that she would keep them indoors. The rental space was a structure attached to the side of the home. It had a bathroom and a bedroom with a microwave but no kitchen. I asked the lady if there was a way to cook our own meals if we wanted to. She said there was a small camp gas stove and a barbecue grill on the patio we could use. The window to the room we were in looked out onto the patio. Malo and I decided to cook some food in order to save on the cost of eating out for the duration of our short vacation.

We went onto the patio and began cutting and chopping when all of a sudden we saw the first black cat. We froze and waited for it to walk past us. It finally did and we continued, wondering why I chose a rental with a cat. Just then another black cat came from inside the main house. We were sure it was not the same one since we had not seen it circle back into the house.

How many cats do they have here anyway? We wondered.

Instead of walking by, the cat walked toward us. We gasped and held our breaths in terror. Malo was sitting on a stool, so she snatched her legs upward, away from the ground. I was standing and felt the cat close to my legs. It rubbed its body against my legs, and I felt my flight-or-fight instinct kick in. Soon enough the cat sauntered away. Malo and I were beginning to rethink our idea to cook on the patio. We kept one eye on our chopping and slicing and another on the cats' whereabouts.

One of the cats returned to where we were and came close enough that we had to pause as we contemplated our escape. All of a sudden it jumped onto the sink we were working on. We both screamed and ran off. Malo made a dash for the room while I ran in the opposite direction. I made my way back into the room, and Malo and I burst into laughter at our silliness. I sent a text message to the lady of the house and asked her to kindly get her cats inside the house so we could cook in peace. Thankfully, she did, and I went out to finish the rest of the cooking. Malo refused to return to the patio, saying she did not trust those cats not to be let out again. She would finish her own portion of the cooking using the microwave, she insisted. Since we did not have enough pots, it took us way more than we had anticipated to finish the cooking. By the time we were done, it was nightfall, and we were too tired to eat much.

I once heard someone tell me she had a pet mouse. My look of shock must have told her what I thought about that. Mice are seen as pests in my country. I have memories of my mom raising an alarm whenever she found a mouse in the house. We all had to stop what we were doing and try to kill it. Killing mice usually involved a lot of hysteric screeches and object throwing. On one hand, you're scared to have it jump at you. On the other, you're determined to get rid of it. There is no catching a mouse just to set it free like I've seen people do in America. Why set it free only for it to find its way back indoors to destroy clothes and documents? I've come to see that animals we consider a source of meat and those we see as disgusting, are pets here. Namely goats and lizards, respectively. I wouldn't even get on an elevator if there was a someone with a dog in it. I'd rather wait for the elevator to return or take the stairs. I often cross to the other side of the road just to avoid someone walking with a dog. That's how uncomfortable I am around dogs. I am not planning to ever visit anyone who has a reptile in their house, either.

Besides the difference in animal interactions between Nigeria and the US, gift receiving or giving was unusual for me. Sure, we gave people birthday gifts on their birthdays and exchanged gifts during Christmas, but our gift sharing culture has nothing on the American one, especially during Christmas. The only thing I remember receiving from my parents during the Christmas holiday was a new digital wristwatch. Somehow that seemed to be a recurring yearly gift. Even when they would ask me what I wanted, I would say a wristwatch.

One time, I got a new Bible for a Christmas gift. I can't remember if I'd asked for it or if they had just thought it would be a good gift at the time. Typically, when we receive gifts in Nigeria, we take them home and then open them, even if we'd received it at someone else's house. We can then call or text to express our thanks or save our thanks for the next time we meet in person. Not so in the US.

My experience is that when Americans give you gifts, they expect you to open it right there. My brother describes it as "...people watching you with eagle eyes waiting to see your reaction to their gift."

I don't always express my feelings, and I've been told I can be hard to read sometimes. So, when I'm made to open gifts in front of onlookers, I often don't have a lot of expression on my face. I would usually smile in gratitude, but somehow I always feel I disappoint the giver by not being more expressive. I wonder if they feel like they made a terrible gift choice even though I probably loved the gift and couldn't wait to use it. It is such an awkward situation for me to be in, but I've been learning to adapt to that part of the American culture since I have a wonderful mother-in-law who loves to give gifts. And I genuinely believe she gives the best gifts. Thankfully, she understands the awkwardness I feel in being the center of attention and allows me the freedom of opening gifts in my own private time. I also try to understand the culture and push through some of that awkwardness enough to open some gifts even with other people looking on. I still cannot guarantee that my facial expression will match the delight I feel at receiving a great gift, though.

I'm always baffled at how much of a credit society America is. People pay for expensive cars, clothes, and whatever else that they cannot afford because they have the ability to put it all on a credit card. I personally find it difficult to buy things I cannot pay for right away. The only exceptions would be tuition and mortgage. Anything else can wait till I am able to pay it off at the time of purchase. But that's just me and how I operate based on my mom's influence. I'm now at a point in my life where I am completely debt-free, and I do not take it for granted. I know all too well how it feels to be in debt, so having transitioned from a struggling graduate student to a financially stable professional, I'm not about to walk myself into any sort of unnecessary debt.

Another thing that strikes me as odd is how dependent the American culture is on drugs. I don't mean the hard stuff like cocaine, heroin, and opioids even though there is a lot of addiction to those too, among certain groups. I'm referring to drugs in general. There seems to be a drug for everything, and people seem very quick to turn to medications before anything else. Caffeine is the wake-up drug in many Western countries, and America is not exempt. I've heard people say things like, "I can't have any conversation until I've had my morning coffee," which I find utterly ridiculous. When I wake up in the mornings and hit the shower, the water on my face is enough to wake me up for the rest of the day, no matter the level of tiredness I feel. There's nothing wrong with daily caffeine intake. I just find it strange, is all.

Pregnancy comes with many challenges as any woman who's been through at least one pregnancy will tell you. The changes a woman's body goes through, the discomfort as her belly swells day after day, and the cravings. When I was pregnant with my daughter, I craved Nigerian food. I wished I could somehow teleport myself to Nigeria and enjoy all the local foods. I experienced all-day nausea and vomiting for the entire first trimester. Nothing would stay down. I had to factor in vomiting time into my morning routine before work. It was a tough trimester. I was too nauseous to cook my own meals and nothing else seemed appealing. I began to lose weight since I wasn't able to keep anything down. I lost ten pounds in the first trimester.

I learned of a cook in the UK who cooked Nigerian stews and soups. I reasoned that if I had stew and soup I could always find other foods to couple them with. Stews and soups are the bedrock of any Nigerian meal. Stews can be combined with rice, yams, or bread. Soups can be coupled with *eba* (a meal made from dried, grated cassava), pounded yam, or *fufu* (a meal made from maize flour). I figured if I had those I would be all set. I could easily get yams, bread, and rice from the grocery stores. I shouldn't say easily because I often have to drive an hour to get to the store that carries the type of bread I like, and African yams are not readily available in *white* New Hampshire. I reached out to the cook, and ordered *ayamase* stew, a local delicacy in Nigeria and a tomato-based soup. It took a couple of weeks, but it finally arrived.

I was eager to finally have some authentic Nigerian stew, but I was sorely disappointed. I wanted to cry. It was not even the wasted money spent ordering food all the way from the UK that was so painful. It was the huge let down after the anticipation of finally having access to delicious Nigerian food. There were tiny stones in the stew, which I discovered during lunch at work one day. I had been looking forward to lunch only to chew stones with each bite of my rice and stew. My friend, Chinwe, had also ordered some soup, so we had both placed a joint order so as to split the shipping costs. The soup she had ordered had arrived almost sour. We did not hesitate to email the cook about our disappointment with the meal. From reviews, we saw that she delivered to many countries across the world, and all the reviews had been positive. I was tempted to go on her Instagram page to leave an honest, albeit, negative review but I decided against it. It was not worth the effort. It would have been an angry review given my disappointment since my hopes had been dashed into pieces. It had been a wasted effort at trying to secure Nigerian food. It was a traumatizing experience in a way because after that, each time I saw a picture of or heard about *ayamase* stew, all I remembered was chewing stones.

My husband suggested we go to the Nigerian church that was a few minutes' drive from our apartment. We had driven by it several times. There had to be someone there who knew a Nigerian caterer, he reasoned. He volunteered to attend a church service there the next Sunday after which he would casually inquire about a caterer. I thought visiting the church for a three-hour service just to make an inquiry was a little overkill, and I said as much. I suggested that it was better to drop by at the end of their service and make my inquiries. My husband thought that was too direct. Nigerians are nothing if not direct, I pointed out.

We picked out a Sunday, and he dropped me off at the door. I could still hear preaching going on upstairs. It was about 12:30 in the afternoon. Their Sunday service was supposed to be over by 12 according to their signpost outside the church. I went up the stairs and saw a woman nursing her baby in the hallway. I greeted her and told her I was just there to see if anyone knew any caterer they could refer me to. If she was surprised by my question, she did not show it. She told me to ask one of the ushers, gesturing towards the congregation. I thanked her and made my way toward the open door to my right.

I could see people seated and hear someone preaching. A man came toward me and asked how he could help. I told him what I was there for, and he went in to get another usher. Again, I repeated what my mission there was. "My wife is a caterer!" he exclaimed. He asked me what my name was and from his name I could tell we were from the same tribe. "She is not here now because she had to work the late-night shift last night, but I can call her now to see if she is awake. If she is you can go to my house and meet with her."

I said, "Sure!"

He called his wife and within minutes, he was giving me his home address. My husband and I headed toward his home. His wife happened to be a very friendly and jovial woman. She welcomed us warmly. I explained my first trimester struggles to her, and she was very sympathetic. She had experienced similar aversion to food during her own pregnancies. Her oldest son looked to be in his teenage years so although that was a long time ago, she said the experience was still vivid in her mind.

She said she worked as a nurse, but she used to be a caterer back in Nigeria. She had recently just been thinking of picking it back up as a side gig. She asked me what I wanted to have her cook for me. I asked her what type of things she would be able to cook. She said, "Anything you want." She mentioned that she had just made some food for her family and asked if I wanted to try some as a sample. I nodded yes. She gave us a plate and two spoons. My husband looked puzzled for a moment. I realized I hadn't yet told him about the interesting tradition in my tribe where a married couple is generally expected to eat from the same plate. I'm not sure if this is a common practice in other tribes in Nigeria, but it is supposed to be a sign of unity although it is not always practical. My husband is vegetarian, and I love meat so we eat different foods that cannot be on the same plate.

Eating a meal made by a Nigerian that was not me was exactly what I needed at that point in my pregnancy. My husband had tried to cook meals for me early on, which I had appreciated, but his culinary skills, when it came to Nigerian foods, were sorely lacking, and we were both frustrated. Him, at what he believed was my constant criticism of his attempts at cooking, and me, at what I saw as him not paying attention to exactly how much water and seasoning I wanted in my noodles for it to go down easy. Even though nine times out of ten, it ended up finding its way back up my throat before it could settle in my stomach anyway. The feeling of noodles coming back up is absolutely weird, I can tell you that.

We were both relieved to have someone else do the cooking for the time being. She made stews, soups, jollof rice, fried rice, *puff puff*—whatever

I wanted. I would tell her what I wanted, and she would tell me what it would cost. Of course, as a Nigerian, I would always try to bargain for a lower price.

The second trimester was easier: I threw up only twice. Two weeks before my due date, my mom arrived. Oh, my blessed mama. Was a girl ever so happy to see her mommy? I was happy to let the caterer know my mama was in town, and I would not be needing her services any longer. Maybe until the next baby, but I like to think I'll be better prepared then.

My mom took over the cooking, and I'm pretty sure most of the pregnancy weight I gained happened in those last two weeks before the baby came. I planned to work up until I went into labor, so my mom would wake up extra early to make me meals to take to work. Given the timing of the onset of nausea, I had to eat every two to three hours to avoid being sick and dizzy at work, so I had two different meals and a snack. That was another challenging part of pregnancy for me. In my non-pregnant state, I could get away with eating two to three times a day, and I was fine. I never snacked. If I snack in between meals, then I would not be able to eat the next meal since I won't be hungry enough. I learned the hard way that I could not get away with that while pregnant, especially in the first trimester. I was sometimes able to get away with not eating every two hours in the third trimester, but the sudden ringing in my ears and blurry vision would remind me when I've gone too long without replenishment. Very inconvenient. I was glad to have my mom around to pamper me as we prepared for the arrival of our baby.

One of the traditions we have in my tribe is the naming ceremony. As the name implies, it is a ceremony in which a new baby is given his or her names. It takes place exactly seven days after the baby is born. A Yoruba child in Nigeria can have up to ten names. I remember my youngest brother's naming ceremony. I was eleven at the time and I knew all the ten names. Now, I only remember four of them. Usually grandparents would be asked to bring names that they would like to give to the new baby. But the names the parents select is what the child goes by and what goes on the birth certificate.

The name giving responsibility differs among families. For example, my first name was given by my mother's mother, while my brother's first name was given by my father's mother. Our middle names came from our parents. Although I am not always a fan of many of the cultural practices within my tribe, I wanted to do a naming ceremony for my baby so we informed our friends and family and we ended up doing a modified-to-American style, traditional naming ceremony. It was the best naming ceremony I have ever attended, although I may be biased. My father-in-law, who had never attended a Nigerian naming ceremony, did a quick research on what it was about, and he presided over the ceremony perfectly.

When I was younger, I used to think that as soon as I left my country, I was going to turn my back to my culture and the enslavement it encouraged, especially toward women. But being older now, I actually enjoy sharing parts of my culture with other people, as well as talking about my culture, even the annoying parts of it. I used to think I did not want my future children to have any part in my culture since I was constantly annoyed by it as a young girl in Nigeria. Now having had a child of my own, I want her to know where her mother came from. I want her to know her mother's roots and feel a connection to them.

There are many clichés Nigerian parents are known for. One is when children ask to go to Mr. Biggs, KFC, or any of the fast food restaurants, the average Nigerian parent would respond with: "There is rice at home." I've also heard of some Nigerian parents sticking flight tickets on their refrigerator, particularly those who migrated to Western countries and are raising their kids in countries that have different sets of values and methods for raising children. Whenever their children misbehave, they remind them that "there is a one-way ticket back to Nigeria waiting for you." There are so many of these clichés, and my understanding is that these are not unique to Nigerian parents—they extend to other parts of Africa.

As a Nigerian parent, I cannot wait to say to my kids: "There is rice at home," whenever they are clamoring for fast food.

Regardless of all the peculiarities of the American culture, and the challenges in finding foods I can eat, I have learned a lot from living in this country. I find it to be a great country full of opportunities. One thing that stands out to me about the US is that if one works hard and keeps striving for more, one would be successful. I grew up and lived among hard workers. Lagos is filled with hard workers. Market women are usually up as early as 4 a.m., if not earlier—without coffee, I might add. Bus drivers and bus conductors are usually the first groups of people up and about in the city on any given day. Although most places of employment resume at 8, most workers are out as early as 5 a.m. to beat the traffic. I've had to leave home at 4.30 a.m. just to get to work by 8. The terrible roads and bad traffic usually because what would have been a thirty-minute ride to become a three-hour journey. Nigeria is filled with hard workers, but the terrible state of the economy (caused by the negligence of those in power), wasteful use of our taxes, and the lack of electricity all contribute to sabotage the efforts of the middle class such that by the end of the day, there's not a lot left to show for all their hard work.

Sometimes I love my home country, other times I hate it. It seems nothing works there. Living in America has taught me that hard work does pay off—even if many immigrants have to work many times as hard. It's refreshing to see the fruits of one's labor and the results of one's efforts. Living in America has encouraged me to keep striving for a more fulfilling life and has encouraged me to position myself for newer and more empowering opportunities.

Most importantly, living in America brought me some of the best things in my life—an incredibly loving husband, an amazing daughter, and great in-laws.

A FAITH-BASED JOURNEY

WE'RE ALL PRODUCTS OF OUR pasts, upbringing, and personal beliefs. Our pasts and upbringing have a profound way of shaping our minds one way or another.

Anyone who's known me since I was in my late teens knows I had a preference on the kind of man I wanted to marry. More specifically, the race of the man I wanted to marry. I'm not sure where this preference came from. All I know is that one afternoon when I was nineteen, I walked up to my mom and said, "I don't want to marry a Nigerian or an African." My mom looked at me like I was drunk. I continued, "I want to marry a foreigner. It doesn't matter where he is from as long as he is not African."

I told my father the same and he told me I was being silly. As a young girl in Nigeria, I was constantly annoyed by the patriarchy I witnessed all around me. To give an example of what we have to deal with, picture a woman who goes to visit her parents with her husband. She and her husband are both relaxed. Her parents ask them what they'd like to eat and drink. Lunch is served. Everyone is happy. Her mother refuses to let her or her husband clean the dishes afterward, saying they're her guests in her home and urges them to relax. The same couple visit the husband's parents' home. The atmosphere is slightly different. Her in-laws appear welcoming. It's time for lunch, but the wife can sense some tension. The cultural expectation is that she goes into the kitchen to help cook and also to clean up after. If she chooses to sit as the guest that she is, that's enough reason to set the gossip mill rolling. If she has a sister-in-law, she'll probably get some side eye and mumblings. Then the mother-in-law and sister-in-law think, "She thinks she's better than us. She can't even lift a finger, but she's happy to eat our food. How did our son/brother marry such a lazy woman?"

It's typical in African culture for men to be treated like kings and for women to be treated like slaves. Men are raised to think they have no business cooking or helping out with house chores. The absurdity of that never fails to baffle me. A foreign woman married to a Nigerian man can obtain permanent resident status in Nigeria, but a foreign man married to a Nigerian woman cannot do the same. Talk about second-class citizens. I hope that as women begin to understand their rights and come into the knowledge of their own power, more people will start to realize that men and women are indeed equal.

The things I observed growing up made me long for something different. I read about Western countries and things women were able to do there. Although there's still a long way to go for equality between the sexes, even in the Western world, it's gone a lot further in developed countries than in developing ones. I knew I wanted out of the shackles of African society. I wanted to travel the world and broaden my mind. Many of these cultural beliefs and practices are so ingrained in the minds of Africans that many find it difficult to let go of them even when they are faced with a better way of life that exposes the fallacy of these archaic beliefs and how harmful they actually are. It has been refreshing to meet other Africans that are passionate about inspiring change in their homelands, however small.

Being a Christian, I don't embark on possibly life-changing adventures without seeking God's guidance through prayer. I believed I was being led through a different path, and I chose to act in faith and follow that path even when I was unsure of what the destination was. And, oh, what faith it took to leave all that I knew behind to journey to a strange land with even stranger cultures and practices. To let myself believe that my struggles and perseverance would all be worth it in the end. To let myself love and be loved by a man who's as different from me as I am from him. A man who I respect and who respects me. A man who cheers me on as I spread my wings, who supports many of my incredulous ideas, who is not threatened by my big dreams and most importantly, who encourages me to be the woman God has called me to be. This path also brought me an incredible mother-in-law who is generosity personified. She supports me, prays for me, and treats me like her daughter.

The blessings I've encountered on this challenging path are too numerous to count. I moved out of Bethany House in February of 2017 into an apartment I was going to share with my husband after our wedding a month away. This was my first time living by myself since I came to the US, and it was amazing. I had my own privacy; I had my own kitchen and bathroom which I did not have to share with anybody. At least for the next month. Shortly before leaving Bethany House, we were told that the ministry that owned it was planning to close that branch and sell off the house. They said they felt they were being called to focus on a different type of ministry. I was stunned. The house, its location, and all it stood for had been very valuable to all of us girls who lived there and those who had lived there before us. The house had been established in 1890 with the purpose of being a home away from home and providing support for young women to achieve their educational and professional goals. I couldn't help but think that God had ordered my steps perfectly. *What are the chances that the house was still open when I needed it most, and when I was ready to leave and move on, the owners were also ready to move on to other ventures?*

The journey of a thousand miles begins with a single step. This famous Chinese proverb is as true for me as it is for anybody. If anyone wants to do anything, whether it is starting over in a country, starting a new and seemingly intimidating project, or turning away from the status quo, it all starts with one step of faith. I can't help but wonder how my many steps of faith have led me to this point in my life, which I'm very thankful for. Yet, I'm only just beginning.

In a few months, I'll be taking an oath of allegiance to become a US citizen, but even as I think of becoming an American, I like to think I'll always be 100% Nigerian.

The end.

REFERENCES

1. United States Census Bureau. Selected Sub-Saharan African and Caribbean Ancestry Groups Making Their Mark: Nigerians Outpace U.S. Educational and Occupational Levels. Available at: https://www.census.gov/newsroom/press-releases/2017/cb17-108-subsaharan.html Published June 28, 2017. Accessed December 12, 2019

2. Casmir L. BACHELOR'S AND BEYOND: Data show Nigerians the most educated in the U.S. *Houston Chronicle*. Available at: https://www.chron.com/news/article/Data-show-Nigerians-the-most-educated-in-the-U-S-1600808.php Updated January 12, 2018. Accessed December 12, 2019.

3. Lin LY, Sidani JE, Shensa A, et al. ASSOCIATION BETWEEN SOCIAL MEDIA USE AND DEPRESSION AMONG U.S. YOUNG ADULTS. *Depress Anxiety*. 2016;33(4):323–331. doi:10.1002/da.22466

4. Twenge JM, Joiner TE, Rogers M L, et al. Increases in Depressive Symptoms, Suicide-Related Outcomes, and Suicide Rates Among U.S. Adolescents After 2010 and Links to Increased New Media Screen Time. *Clinical Psychological Science*. 2018;6(1):3–17. https://doi.org/10.1177/2167702617723376

www.ingramcontent.com/pod-product-compliance
Lightning Source LLC
Chambersburg PA
CBHW071347080526
44587CB00017B/3006